Praise for *Get the Behavior You Being the Parent You Hate!*

"As a TV host and Mom, I have interviewed many parenting experts. I appreciate straightforward information that I can apply the same day, and that's what I get from Dr. G. She is the on-call expert who gives bite-sized advice with big results. Her medical training coupled with her sense of humor and four kids of her own help me trust *and* like her! This book is chock full of her great advice, along with stories that help me remember what she recommends. I love having her on our show, and you'll love having her on your nightstand!"

—Val Warner, co-host of *Windy City LIVE*

"Truly comprehensive, humorous, and full of practical wisdom, *Getting the Behavior You Want … Without Being the Parent You Hate!* will help put the day-to-day challenges of parenting into perspective, whether you've got toddlers or teens…. As someone who has been a parent I hate from time to time, I highly recommend this book to parents-to-be, parents in crisis, and parents who just want to feel like they can make a difference in their children's lives."

—Deesha Philyaw, co-author of *Co-Parenting 101: Helping Your Kids Thrive in Two Households After Divorce*

"Dr. G. successfully, succinctly, and with a touch of humor answers the question on every parent's mind: 'How can I give my kids what they need, while they whine for what they want?' Her book is full of advice and practical how-to-tips on how to guide your children's behavior to build what she calls the 3 R's: respect, responsibility and resilience…. Her ultimate goal: to teach children (toddler to age 12) compassion and charity and to raise a generation that can look beyond themselves. I believe with this book in hand, parents have a shot at achieving this goal."

—Estelle Erasmus, president, board of directors, Mothers & More, Huffington Post contributor, and contributor to *What Do Mothers Need? Motherhood Activists and Scholars Speak Out on Maternal Empowerment for the 21st Century*

"As a travel nanny I work with all kinds of families and deal with all kinds of behavior. Parents want practical ideas to 'get the job done,' not a lot of philosophy. *Get the Behavior You Want … Without Being the Parent You Hate* delivers down-to-earth advice, examples, and clear guidelines. Dr. G makes it easy to identify your goals and how to accomplish them. And, I love that she breaks her advice down into age appropriate categories. You'll use this book for years to come."

—Donna Robinson, The Traveling Nanny, 2008 Nanny of the Year

"An in-the-trenches primer of real live opportunities and situations [to teach responsibility, respect, and resilience] told with humor and compassion by a woman raising four boys. From teaching table manners to the proper address of adults, chores to money management, and how to address boredom, aggression and those 'life is not fair' moments, Dr. G provides a wealth of practical observation, advice and how-to suggestions. If the future you see for your children includes a successful launch as a young adult, and you are not sure how to get from here to there, pick up this book today. You won't regret it."

—Kathy Webb, in-home childcare expert and co-founder,
HomeWork Solutions, Inc.

Also by Deborah Gilboa, MD:

Teach Respect: That's My Kid! 50 Activities for Parents to Do with Children

Teach Responsibility: Empower Kids with a Great Work Ethic! 50 Tasks for Children

Teach Resilience: Raising Kids Who Can Launch! 50 Actions Parents Can Use

Get the Behavior You Want ... Without Being the Parent You Hate!

Dr. G's Guide to Effective Parenting

Deborah Gilboa, MD

demosHEALTH

NEW YORK

Visit our website at www.demoshealth.com

ISBN: 978-1-936303-71-7
e-book ISBN: 978-1-61705-214-9

Acquisitions Editor: Julia Pastore
Compositor: diacriTech

Front cover photo: Becky Thurner Braddock

Medical information provided by Demos Health, in the absence of a visit with a health care professional, must be considered as an educational service only. This book is not designed to replace a physician's independent judgment about the appropriateness or risks of a procedure or therapy for a given patient. Our purpose is to provide you with information that will help you make your own health care decisions.

The information and opinions provided here are believed to be accurate and sound, based on the best judgment available to the authors, editors, and publisher, but readers who fail to consult appropriate health authorities assume the risk of injuries. The publisher is not responsible for errors or omissions. The editors and publisher welcome any reader to report to the publisher any discrepancies or inaccuracies noticed.

Library of Congress Cataloging-in-Publication Data

Gilboa, Deborah.
    Get the behavior you want—without being the parent you hate! : Dr. G's guide to effective parenting / Deborah Gilboa, MD.
        pages cm
    Includes index.
    ISBN 978-1-936303-71-7
    1. Parenting. 2. Parent and child. I. Title.
    HQ755.8.G5167 2014
    649'.1—dc23
                                        2014010813

Special discounts on bulk quantities of Demos Health books are available to corporations, professional associations, pharmaceutical companies, health care organizations, and other qualifying groups. For details, please contact:

Special Sales Department
Demos Medical Publishing, LLC
11 West 42nd Street, 15th Floor
New York, NY 10036
Phone: 800-532-8663 or 212-683-0072
Fax: 212-941-7842
E-mail: specialsales@demosmedical.com

Printed in the United States of America by McNaughton & Gunn.
14 15 16 17 18 / 5 4 3

*Let's face it. It takes a lot of chutzpah to write a parenting book
while you are parenting someone.
Or have parents.
Or even know parents.
To Arthur Goldberg and Bernice Goldberg, who gave me
all I needed.
To Noam Gilboa, who knows me best and still chooses me, and
To Ari and Nadav and Oren and Gavri
(in order of appearance)
whom we are blessed to parent, and manage to test every idea
we have
about what that means.
To family made, and family found.*

*And to all the parents I know. You are the parenting experts on
your kids, and
I'm grateful our kids get to keep fixing the world together.*

Contents

Part III: Resilience: Raising Problem Solvers

Part IV: Making Change Happen: How to Actually Get Kids to *Do* This Stuff

Introduction

I am a parenting expert on the four kids who live in my house. You? Are a parenting expert on the kids who live in your home! No one knows the kids you love better, or cares more about their welfare, than you do. Even better, you are perfectly placed to raise those kids up to be adults you genuinely admire. You guide their behavior and choices as they progress from toddler to teen.

But *how* do we actually do this parenting stuff?

Well, I've nagged, yelled at, threatened, and guilted my children to try to get them to behave well. Not all of the time, and usually not on purpose, but, just like many parents, I've done all this and more. Not only do I feel really horrible about it afterwards, but (and here is the kicker) it doesn't work.

My husband and I are raising four boys. There are six years between the oldest and the youngest and we get a lot of sympathetic glances from strangers when we're in public. You can actually see people trying to figure out if we maybe got surprised by twins or something, because clearly no one would do this on purpose! But we actually couldn't wait to have a big family, and most days it's excellent. Chaos for sure, but excellent.

In addition to 24/7 parenting, I am a family doctor. I am privileged to care for hundreds of families, most with young children and teenagers. I work with families facing true horrors like cancer or muscular dystrophy; families fractured by circumstance or action; families challenged by legal, financial, and emotional stressors. I have families that look "normal" or even "perfect." Here is what I've learned: Everyone struggles with parenting. Everyone.

Picture your kids grown into the adult children you'd like to visit in 25 years. That's the prize, right? Adults you've raised that are a comfort to you, raising your grandchildren and leading interesting lives that you get to hear about and take some part in, but with most of the heavy lifting behind you. That's the prize to keep in mind during your challenges. Think about raising an adult you will respect and *like*, and want to be around. What character traits, knowledge, and skills do children need to become those adults? How can you encourage them to be responsible enough to someday be financially independent? What lessons will help them respect themselves and others? How can you guide them toward the resilience they will need when they are met by life's challenges?

Because of my work as a family doctor, I get invited to speak in my community, and everyone wants to talk about raising kids. As these speaking invitations have moved farther from home, I've been most surprised by what doesn't change: the issues adults face as we try to guide the children in our care. From New York to Thailand to Israel and back to California, I'm asked the same question: "How can I give my kids what they *need* while they whine for what they *want*?"

Picture your children today. Can you see the obstacles that lie between how they behave now and the adults you want to help them become? The good news is that time will take care of some of these behaviors without any intervention. Very few college students throw on-the-floor temper tantrums. High schools do not need must-be-toilet-trained policies (quick note: don't stress about toilet training; children eventually figure this out). Kids need life experiences and maturity just like we did. This book is a practical guide to help you shepherd your children from today to a generation from now, creating adults you will want to call your own.

Before I sat down to write a parenting book, I wrote three activity guides. As adults we can be as "empowered" as we'd like by strong philosophies. However, parents, grandparents, nannies, teachers, soldiers, after-school staff, camp directors, every group I've ever addressed has wanted to focus on being effective rather than empowered. What can we *do*? These three 64-page, cell-phone-sized books have 50 different activities, one per page, that adults can do with kids to build respect, responsibility, or resilience.

With these activity guides in hand, parents asked me for a book that would answer their most pressing questions. "I know the traits I want for my children, I see what they need," I hear from parents all over the world. "How can I give them those values and guide their behavior?" Throughout this book you will find answers to these issues, as well as the specific parent questions I hear most often.

How to use this book.

If you have time, you can absolutely just read this book cover to cover. Of course, if you have time to do *that* I think you should put down the book and go back outside to the beach and enjoy the child-free vacation you are obviously missing!

More likely, you are squeezing in a little reading between lots of other activities and responsibilities. You can scan the table of Contents for the part that concerns your family most right now. Each of the four sections deals with one theme of raising mature, admirable kids. Each chapter is meant to address a particular issue in that theme.

Schools teach the "3 R's" to our kids: reading, writing, and arithmetic (yes, I do think it's strange that only one of those starts with "R"). Raising kids centers around a completely different set of 3 R's: respect, responsibility, and resilience. If adults who love kids can give them *these* three R's, we will give them the tools and skills they need to thrive as adults.

The first section is about respect. Teaching your children to respect themselves, to treat you with respect, and to be respectful toward family and other adults in their world is the first element in raising kids who will be able to succeed in whatever they choose to pursue. This will really pave the way for their own happiness, preparing them to choose well and create a loving family of their own.

The second section is about responsibility. Childhood responsibilities are training for adulthood. The ways we (sloooowly) teach our kids to handle their own bodies, homework, chores, sports practice, theater rehearsal, youth group, and so on, as they grow is the best impact we can have on their future job performance.

The third section dives into resilience. How can kids learn how to handle it when things don't go their way? Adversity happens. We need to give our kids the skills to make their way through those challenges and come out stronger on the other side.

Most important thing to know about this book.

The last section is about how to get your kids to actually do all this (and really anything you need them to do) and what to do when they won't. Why isn't this section first? Because this is the hardest part.

If you don't read about some of the great respect and responsibility and resilience your kids can learn before you read this part, it may not seem worth it to struggle through their resistance. The first three sections lay out the goals. This section offers a bunch of different paths to travel in order to get those goals met.

You are already doing a lot of this. As parents, our efforts are always well-intentioned and often right on the mark. This book is to give you new ideas, and provide structure for your consistency. Choose the goals that ring true for your family and pursue those. One at a time usually works best.

My goal is to change the conversations we are having about parenting. Whether I'm talking to a news anchor in Chicago, addressing a huge corporate group for a Fortune 500 corporation, or Skyping with a group of soldiers who are deployed in Afghanistan, everyone wants to know if they should be trying harder to make their kids happy. We need to get off the "happiness hook" we're hung up on as a culture. When we give our kids boundaries we make them unhappy. It's still the right thing to do. When we give our kids the ability to show respect for themselves and others, the responsibility inherent in a strong work ethic, and the resilience to overcome hardship, we hand them the ability to find and make their own happiness for life.

There are a lot of suggestions in this book based on a child's age. These are keeping in mind the developmental abilities for kids who are what's called "neuro-typical." This means they are not on the autism spectrum and do not have cognitive delays of any kind. If your child has special needs, most of these suggestions will work but the age may need to be adjusted based on individual circumstances.

I've included some commonly asked questions throughout the book. You'll see "Ask Doctor G" boxes with concerns I've heard multiple times from parents. Have a question you don't see here? Please get in touch with me!

My favorite thing about parenting in the new millennium is access: access to information, access to strategies and feedback, access to people. Please take advantage of the many ways there are to be in touch. I want to hear how these ideas work out in your home. Contact me through my website, visit any of the 1,327 social media platforms I'm connected to, or come to one of my live events. Send me your experiences so that more parents can be effective when they face what you face. As I develop an online learning series for the schools, camps, and after school programs that are helping us guide our children, I need your input! For a list of the many ways you can get in touch, flip to the About the Author section at the back of the book.

None of this character-building stuff is easy, but some of it is simple. The Peace Corps says it has the toughest job you'll ever love. I have definitely had a few mornings that I'd have preferred a steamy jungle and digging latrines to waking my kids for school. On the upside, I don't think the Peace Corps gets as many hugs.

Take heart! First of all, most adults are pretty good people and every single one of us was a tough kid once upon a time, at least some days. In this book you'll find that there are ways of taking the battles out of your day so you can enjoy your children and think about the bigger picture for each of them. Now: Use this book like a "choose your own adventure" map.

If you've picked this up at a time when things are going smoothly at home, relax and enjoy. There are effective, positive strategies in these pages to strengthen your children's character and give them huge advantages in life. They can amaze you with their abilities to treat themselves and others well, to master new jobs, and to conquer new situations.

If you are feeling frustrated by something that is happening in your home, think about the last week you've spent with your child and anything you'd like to change. Is homework a battle? Tired of eye-rolling or back-talking? Want to encourage your child to eat healthier or be a better family member or help out around the house? Well, here is what doesn't work: nagging, yelling, threatening, and guilt.

Read on and we'll talk about what does work.

You might focus on helping your children to be respectful of you and other adults in their life, of their friends, and also of themselves. Perhaps you're thinking about the responsibilities you want your child to take on. Maybe it's time to teach your children the resilience they need to grow into the best adults they can be. Learn about strategies that will ease or eliminate the big battles in your home.

Get the behavior you want ... without being the parent you hate!

PART I

RESPECT
THAT'S MY KID!

1

Respect: Why Bother?

Respect is the ability to recognize someone's worth or excellence and communicate it.

This section is first for this reason: *How we treat ourselves and others is the most important concept adults can teach children.*

Do your kids recognize your worth? Probably, especially if someone would ask:

- "Is your mom important to you?"
- "Is your dad valuable?"
- "Is there something excellent about your grandparent?"

Children have great, sometimes funny, and often sweet answers to these questions. Ask one over dinner tonight. I dare you.

Do your kids show that they see your worth when they speak to you? That is a lot less common. In our quest to "be real" with our kids, we sacrifice a fair amount of respectful communication. But we don't have to. And more, we do our kids a big disservice when we let them speak and act disrespectfully.

Will you do a little research? Just observe your child's interactions over the next few days. How would you feel if he spoke to a teacher the way he speaks to you? Do you want her friends to treat her the way she behaves toward her siblings? When your child disagrees with you, does she know how to say so without nastiness?

You may be thinking, "Seriously? This is what Dr. G wants me to argue with my kids about?" Seriously. And here is why.

Why this is good for you:

1. **You have value.** If your kids can't (or won't) see that, they can't and won't learn from you. They won't be guided by you; they will spend even more time trying to prove how different they are from you and how little they need you.

2. **When you feel valued it's easier to put up with the hard stuff.** Parenting is often really tough. But it does not have to be thankless, and it shouldn't be. How we feel about work is directly related to how much respect we get for doing that work. Take the time to teach your kids how to communicate their respect, as well as their gratitude. You will have more patience with them and with the demands on your time, energy, and heart.

Why this is good for your kids:

1. **Self-esteem is built on self-respect.** From the time our kids are babies we are told in magazines and books how important it is to build a child's self-esteem. Of course it matters to tell our kids about our love and admiration. However, if kids don't know what it means to respect themselves—their bodies, their personalities, their needs (as opposed to their wants)—they won't be able to take good care of themselves. They won't know that they deserve to be treated well.

2. **Self-respect gives children the power to walk away from disrespect.** Want your children to pick good friends? Expect your kids to resist negative peer pressure? How do you teach them to avoid abusive relationships? They have to recognize the difference between respectful and disrespectful treatment, and know that one is good and one is bad.

3. **Showing respect is a skill that takes time to learn.** We often feel respect without coaching (though reminders don't hurt kids at all). Showing it is another matter. I don't know about you, but I'm most often snarky and irritable with the people who are most important to me.

4. **Respect opens adult ears, and minds.** Most adults are quick to say "No" to kids. And most kids are pretty disrespectful to grown-ups. This may be bad news for our society, but, well, that's a different book. As parents we only have to worry about our own kids. The great news here is that we can give our kids a HUGE advantage among their peers when we teach these skills.

5. **Kids who can communicate respectfully get what they want.** Let's be honest. We want our kids to get most of what they want, especially as they grow up. One kindergartner calls out, "I want a cookie!" Another says, "Ms. Matthews, may I please have a cookie?" Who do you think is getting that cookie first? If your child wants to be on a certain team, or get a particular part in the play, a good grade, or even a job, you're usually rooting for them. Rather than jumping in to "fix" each situation later, give your kids this leg up on the competition NOW!

The following chapters in this section will help you raise kids who can feel and show respect for themselves and for everyone they encounter.

2

Who's Got Your Vote to Run the House?

Who's in charge at your house? I don't mean who is paying the bills—grown-ups are stuck with that for sure. I mean, who sets the tone for each day? Whose mood has the most sway over the way your morning goes? Let me give you a sense of why this question is so important.

When I walk into an exam room for a well-child checkup I know right away who is in charge. AJ is balancing on my seat with one foot, mushy granola bar in one hand, blood pressure cuff in the other, trying to see if the cord will help him spin faster. Keira is coloring in her book (and on the curtain) while poking her younger sister with her toe. Matthew is trying to block his mom's view of the computer so that his older brother can find a video game for them to play—it's nice to see siblings working together, right? But I'm not looking at the younger ones to figure out how things are in this family.

Perhaps you read that trying to figure out who was most like your child, and who I think the "good kid" is. Or you were waiting for me to compare this to the child who is waiting patiently with the preplanned activities or snacks that the excellent parent has brought along. Guess what? That never actually happens.

Here is the secret that a lot of parents don't guess: the mood in the room doesn't depend on the child. After 10 minutes (on a great day!) of waiting in a boring doctor's office, the kids are usually causing a little mischief. The differences depend on the parents. Not so much on the words they use: "Get down, now ... Be careful ... That isn't ours ... Don't touch that ... I said no!" The difference is in parents' belief in themselves. The mother who says, "I said no!" might mean, "I said no and you and I both know if I have to remind you again you won't like the consequences." Or she might mean, "I said no and I know you're not going to listen but I don't know what else to do." I'm not the only one in the room that hears that difference—the child is very clear about what "I said no" means. It's this understanding (not the actual words) that help that child decide whether or not to listen. If you don't expect to be obeyed they will meet your expectations.

So back to the exam room. If AJ's parent is pulling him off the stool and taking away the BP cuff with the absolute certainty that as soon as they let go he is going to climb back up or do something more unmanageable, then that is what he'll do.

The trick is to know two things:

1. What consequences your children will face if they don't follow your rules, and

2. That (though it may take a while) they will learn to follow those rules.

So AJ's parent can say firmly, "That is not OK, AJ. It's time to let go and get down. If you can't do that I will help you but then ..." What gets filled in there depends on your child's age and temperament, and your temperament as well. You might say, "We can't tell each other silly stories" or "We'll have to go straight home" or "I won't be able to tell the doctor how well you're behaving." Whatever you say, though, you have to stick with it. More on that later.

- As parents, we know we are in charge of our kids. For some number of years, we are, actually, the boss of them. Don't shy away from that power, but *use that power for good*.

- As parents, we should respect our children. That means we value their excellence and worth. We show them our respect by honoring our roles, and theirs, in our family.

- As parents, we have to teach our children to respect us. Their love comes naturally, but respect has to be learned.

So what, exactly, am I asking you to do?

Be in charge.

No matter what the style and culture of your home—laid back, very organized, lots of joking around, stay-at-home parent, or working three jobs—you can be in charge. You and your parenting partner can be the final judge of what activities are allowed, what behavior is acceptable, and what words can and can't be used in your family.

"Will my kids hate me?" Sometimes. And those days are really hard, but they are worth it. Because, if you're not in charge at your house, your child is. Ever seen how Peter Pan takes charge of his Lost Boys? Someone will step up and set the tone in your family if you don't. Someone is influencing the way everyone treats each other. Don't you want that person to be one or both parents?

"Is this really necessary?" It genuinely is. If you could see how messy my house is, you'd know that I am basically a pretty lazy person. If the effort needed to make our kids speak and act respectfully wasn't going to make an enormous difference in our home, and in the people our kids will grow up to be, I would not bother.

- **Be confident.** Confident that your child will respect you and learn to follow your rules. Know that you are the grown-ups; that you and your partner will decide what is important and which behaviors are acceptable.

- **Be happy.** You have great kids that *often* want to please you. Adventurous or shy, at times bored, occasionally interested in the world around them, thoughtful or self-involved, none of that makes kids "bad" or "hard." Most kids and teens want their parents to be happy for lots of reasons. We'll talk about how to tap into those reasons.

- **Be in charge in your family.** I'm not suggesting that you or your partner be mean or unreasonable. I'm recommending that you make sure that you embrace your parental superpowers and use them for good.

Superpowers? What superpowers? You have the power to help your children feel great about themselves. To rescue them from most danger. To arm them to face all the challenges ahead of them knowing that they are loved and supported and that they won't get away with bad behavior. You teach your children what is right and wrong and how to figure out the differences.

As a parent, this starts with not being afraid of your children. It is OK to be afraid *for* them on occasion, or to dread their bad behavior in a formal situation (even remembering that bad behavior is a normal part of childhood). Don't be afraid that they will be angry with you or act out or say things you don't want to hear. They will. Be in charge anyway! Take all the grief they can dish out and be confident—they will learn to be more respectful, more responsible, and more resilient. This home is yours to make, so make it a place you want to be.

3

Teaching the Skill of Self-Respect

Self-respect means knowing your own worth, and valuing that. Why should we teach this? Three great reasons:

1. Self-respect allows us to get our needs met.

2. Showing others respect is much easier and more genuine when we respect ourselves.

3. Self-respect is a crucial part of the foundation kids need to make good decisions.

Getting our needs met.

Imagine your second-grader sitting at school. She's in math and the teacher has had it with requests for water, bathroom breaks, and so on. The teacher says, "No one else may be excused for the 15 minutes we have left in class. Do your work!" Suddenly, your daughter's stomach cramps and she gets that absolute certainty that she needs the bathroom *immediately*! It takes self-respect to decide that her need to get to the bathroom is more important than (and worth getting in trouble because of) her teacher's command to stay put.

Respect for others grows from self-respect.

Do you want your kids to be respectful toward each person they meet? I do. Of course, that person might be unworthy of respectful behavior at some point. But, up until that time, I want my kids to make a baseline assumption to treat others kindly and respectfully.

Here's an example. I don't want my kids to be racists. I do my darndest not to make assumptions about people based on only what I can see, and I want my kids to give people that same courtesy. So what do I tell them? "Everyone we meet deserves our respect." If my child does not have a healthy sense of self-respect, how can he possibly believe me?

Self-respect leads to stronger decision making.

We give kids a powerful tool when we teach them their own value. This is the foundation they will stand on when they do something different than their friends.

When my son was eight he was invited with three other boys to a birthday party at our local amusement park. He was thrilled, despite the fact that he didn't like rides that go "too high" or "too fast." When he got home we asked how it went. Well, the other boys all wanted to go on the bigger coasters and wanted him to go so they could each have a partner. What did our boy do? "I hung out with the mom while the dad went on the coasters. It was cool." Did the other boys push you to ride? "Yeah, until I asked who wanted me to throw up on them. Then they were fine with it."

It often takes strength of character to go your own way. To speak up if you're hungry, hurt, afraid. To like a class or teacher your peers don't. To be nice to a new kid when the pack has decided he doesn't belong. To enforce your parent's rule about no sneaking snacks even though it's your best friend who asks.

The ability to resist negative peer pressure depends on self-respect.

So how do we teach it?

No matter what your child's age, think about self-respect in terms of his or her feelings and actions. Look for ways that will teach your kids these specific skills:

1. **To recognize their own feelings and needs.** We're not always able or willing to act on a child's needs immediately. That is totally

reasonable. "You just sat at dinner and said you weren't hungry, now you need to wait a half-hour until we are home before you can have a healthy snack." However, we can and should have empathy for a child's feelings even if we're not going to fix the situation for them. The ability to understand how another is feeling, and express it (respectfully), is life-changing.

2. **To connect those feelings to their own behaviors.** When I was growing up, every time I exhibited a behavior that was at all unpleasant, my mother announced that I was "over-tired." It annoyed the heck out of me, but she taught me a basic lesson. If you're having a strong reaction to something, there is the real possibility that more than one factor is at play. Helping our kids to look below a bad feeling for the causes will enable them to change their situation for the better, or at least might *eventually* help them understand when it's time for a nap or a snack.

3. **To value what is excellent or unique about themselves.** OK, I have to say a word here about *what* we value in kids.

   Kids know that they have control over what they do, and not much over what they are, or have, or how they look. Teach kids self-respect by praising and valuing the things they have some responsibility for. That means avoiding phrases like "You're so cute," "What great curly hair you have," and "Wow, you're so tall!"

   It's the process our kids can take real pride in. "You look nice" doesn't feel nearly as great as "You look ready to … (learn, create, lead, discover)." And "Your grades are great" doesn't create the same pride as "I'm impressed with your … (perseverance, dedication, study)." Praising the way our kids play the game is not saying that winning doesn't matter. It will simply teach children to value their own effort and to keep putting it out there.

   What about love? We can and should keep reminding our kids of our love. Don't let that replace value, though. People don't have value because they are loved. Kids who grow up to be adults who measure their value in proof that others love them can make some very bad choices.

What does this three-step education look like?

Toddlers.

➢ **Recognize.** Name feelings. Help them understand what "tired" feels like, and "hungry" and "lonely" and "bored," and so on. The more accurate children learn to be about what they are feeling, the faster they will learn to express that to someone who can help.

➢ **Connect.** Be very concrete. Once you and your toddler identify the problem, work together to find the solution. Then help your toddler notice the change in how she's feeling. "Still hungry?" "No." "That feels better, doesn't it?"

➢ **Value.** Focus on their process. Show pride in a tantrum not thrown, or a quick recovery. Express gratitude for help with a household chore. Verbalize your appreciation for a hug or a hand to hold. Talk about the positive contributions your toddler makes in your family, your neighborhood, or his or her preschool.

ASK DOCTOR G

Parent Q: My little one freaks out about other kids touching her possessions. How can I teach her to share?

*B*efore a playdate, ask your child to bring you two or three items she cannot bear to share. Set those out of sight, and let her know they will come out as soon as the playdate is over. Everything else needs to be shared. If a friend wants a toy, she can say, "Here you go" or "In two minutes," but if she can't share at all you'll play with that child while your daughter sits out for a bit. This teaches her to respect her own needs and address them, but also to behave respectfully toward her friend.

Preschoolers.

➢ **Recognize**. Keep naming those feelings. The more practice kids have at figuring out how they feel, the better they will be at it.

➢ **Connect**. More than one feeling is often at the heart of a tantrum. As your child starts to be able to identify the problem: "He is so mean he took his toy after I had it." Why else? "'Cause I hit him with it?" Oh! Why else? "Because I don't want him to leave." So you're also feeling sad? Good job telling me.

➢ **Value**. What does your preschooler spend time improving? Is he drawing; is she building cool structures? Does she sound out words; does he keep trying for a goal? Kids this age often have more enthusiasm than skill; they'll need that energy to put up with the repetition that skill-building requires.

Elementary schoolers.

➢ **Recognize**. Kids this age have a huge capacity for empathy. Start asking kids about encounters between others. When they notice conflict, ask them to identify the needs and points of view of each side. With whom do they empathize? Why?

➢ **Connect**. What feelings tend to be involved when things don't go well? Do they do their best studying at night or in the morning? How does hunger or fatigue change their behavior? Can they take their own "time-outs" when appropriate to address their own needs?

➢ **Value**. Kids do things to make their world a better place. Praise a child's patience, or curiosity, or initiative. Notice if he is reaching out to include someone socially, or she is showing kindness toward a neighbor or classmate. Does your child walk away from a fight with a sibling rather than engage? Such value!

Middle schoolers.

➢ **Recognize**. This is an age of "re-centering," where kids experience big mood changes and self-centeredness that we often haven't seen since they were toddlers. Take advantage of their improved language skills and ask them to verbalize the emotions and needs that are leading to these bigger tantrums.

➤ **Connect.** Place more responsibility on your tween for acknowledging her feelings and needs without turning those emotions into bad behavior. Kids this age can exercise self-control; they just don't want to.

➤ **Value.** Puberty causes a huge amount of self-consciousness, and a desire to be exactly like their friends at a time when everyone feels different. Instead of arguing with our kids about their diminished self-esteem or insecurities, show empathy for their concern, and challenge them to figure out where they excel. Admire (out loud but *not* in front of their friends) their abilities and character traits that you admire. They don't have to agree with us to hear us.

4

Treat Family Even Better

Remember the glow you felt one time you heard from an adult how well your daughter behaved when you weren't around? That's all it takes, really, to make us feel like, "Wow, I rock this parenting thing!" And occasionally, "Whew, we fooled her!" But sometimes we also think, "Then why doesn't she do that at home?"

It's a tough call. We want our kids' behavior to be excellent when we're not around. First of all, if we're not there we can't steer them in the right direction. Second of all, when they do a good job people like them better. And ... it does make us feel great as parents. Good behavior at a friend's house or on a field trip or in public is proof that some of what we are teaching is getting through. You've taught your son and daughter to say please when asking for something, not to grab, to say thank you or no, thank you. **These lessons are usually learned on friends and their parents but are even more important at home.**

What? Yes, politeness and manners are even more important at home than away. Of the millions of times your children are going to ask for something in the next 10 to 20 years, who are they most often going to be asking? You.

Good manners are the grease that makes everything run more smoothly. I do the laundry once every week (my kids do it a couple of times a week also—more on that later). I don't love it, but it's one of the chores I routinely do at our house. Every time my husband finds clean clothes folded on our bed he thanks me for doing the laundry.

This actively relieves any frustration I feel about this never-ending chore. Years and years and his thanks never get old!

- A spontaneous word of praise or thanks can lighten someone's mood.

- An unsolicited offer to get a snack for a family member when you're getting one for yourself can do more for good relations than any diplomat could accomplish.

- Holding a door makes someone feel noticed.

- Grabbing a package lightens someone's load.

- Asking how someone's day was and listening to the answer makes coming home a pleasure.

All of these are important skills to possess as adults and make home a happier place to be.

ASK DOCTOR G

Parent Q: My son does really well in kindergarten all day and then comes home and behaves terribly, just as I'm trying to get dinner on the table. Why does he only "lose it" for me?

Kids can have a great day at school, or with a babysitter, or at a friend's, and then come home and have a total meltdown. This is actually quite a compliment from your child to you. Seriously, children who know they are loved, who trust their families, show those they trust their true feelings.

Most people relax at home. We give the world a slightly more put together, "OK" version of ourselves, waiting until we are in our own space, with the people who are stuck with us, before we let a bad mood really show. Suppose your child comes home from preschool, or even middle school, with a glowing report and then has a monster tantrum. That happens because home is a totally safe place. Home is where Mom or Dad will love him no matter what.

Ready for the good news? Practicing these skills at home makes them more likely to show up at someone else's house, too. Practice on your partner or other adults in the house; it can only make your relationship even better. Be really polite to your children.

Modeling these behaviors is the fastest way to get your two to seven year olds to try them also.

With older kids, the developmentally normal self-absorption has kicked in and you have to be a little more obvious.

Catch them doing good. When you see any example of new and great manners, jump on it and praise it. Even a teen who rolls her eyes at a goody-goody younger sibling will still want in on a little of that parental admiration. Just remember the teen BS detector—you have to catch kids actually being nice. If you make something up to have something to praise them for, you will lose the point. And don't be afraid to make your expectations clear.

Treat strangers well but treat family even better.

When this feels like one battle too many, consider two facts.

1. Hopefully you have a bunch of years left to live with these people. We should treat the people we spend the most time with best of all.

2. The better a roommate you teach your child to be now, the less likely it is that he will boomerang back as a middle-aged adult needing to live at home again.

5

Spoiler Alert: What You Do Is More Important than How You Feel

Everywhere I go to speak about parenting challenges, I hear this complaint: "Kids today are so entitled!" The question I get over and over is "How can we fix it?"

Entitlement is an attitude—a bad attitude. It's the belief that one deserves to be treated a certain way, just because of who that person is, or what he has. Do you remember what our grandparents called that? Spoiled!

Have you ever had a job with a boss and a paycheck? Imagine you were on your way to that job. Your best friend sent you a snarky text, you had a stomachache, and you realize on the way to work that you left your wallet (with credit card) at the grocery store more than 12 hours ago. Bad day. Do you get to work and toss your stuff into a corner, ignore everyone who speaks to you, blow off your work responsibilities, and focus on texting your friend and calling your credit card company and the store? Do you sulk or snap at your boss and coworkers? If you want to keep your job you don't. You juggle, explain, and squeeze-in some time to deal with the personal while doing your best to handle your work responsibilities.

This represents a very important lesson you learned at some point: what you do is more important than how you feel. You will be judged and rewarded based on your behavior. This is true at work, at school, and in relationships. The words you choose, and the actions you take earn you respect or disdain. The feelings that explain or excuse those actions are rarely taken into account.

Whether or not you think this is a good thing, it is still true in the world. So you owe it to your children to teach them to behave well even when they feel pretty rotten. This starts at home and it starts young.

Looking a little deeper, though, entitlement is based on one underlying certainty. People who act this way believe that how they feel justifies how they behave. For instance:

- I'm late to class because I had a fight with my boyfriend.

- You can't expect me to finish that today—I'm really stressed out.

- I'm blowing off that meeting to hang out with my friends.

- Nasty to the customer? Well, she deserved it! Did you hear how she talked to me?

Every employed, stable adult knows that these kinds of excuses don't fly in the real world. But college professors, employers, even military commanders all tell me they are seeing this unbelievable behavior in young adults.

Where does it start? It starts with the mistaken impression that feelings are more important than actions. Look at the following statement and think about what you want from colleagues, employees, friends, and even your spouse.

How a person acts is more important than how that person feels.

How a person feels does matter. It is important. It's just not *as* important as how that person behaves. The empathy we all crave from others is earned by consistent, respectful behavior.

So how do young adults end up with this misconception? That's easy. We parents don't want our kids to feel the pain of this life lesson, so we protect them.

Our children say things:

- Shut up, Mom!
- I don't want to "be kind." I don't like her!
- You have to write me a note or I'll get in trouble.
- I can't take out the garbage, I'm tired.
- Church today? I don't feel like it.
- Just tell my coach I'm sick or something.
- I don't wanna!

And we say:

- She had a hard day.
- Maybe he's coming down with something.
- I think he's just hungry.
- That child is over-tired.
- It's a phase.
- It's not her fault.

Here's what we can do instead:

1. **Show empathy.** "I care about how you're feeling, and I feel for you in your (exhaustion, frustration, hunger, etc.)." This is how we demonstrate our love to our children.

2. **Stick to our standards.** Our rules for our kids' behavior do not have to change when they don't feel well in some way. "How you act is even more important than how you feel." This is how we demonstrate that we take our parenting seriously. We are willing to enforce the rules and teach them the lessons even when it's hard. Even when they make it harder than it has to be.

ASK◦DOCTOR G

Parent Q: Every time I give my child a chore, he's suddenly "too tired." How am I supposed to argue with that?

You can't argue with that. So offer your son a choice. Is he going up to bed (lights out, no music or electronics) or doing the chore? If this happens, for example, before school? Offer genuine empathy for his extreme fatigue but let him know that he will need to skip all the recreational parts of the evening and go straight to bed after homework is done. He'll go to bed very early, even if he somehow miraculously feels much better. Or you could offer him a longer list of chores to do that evening if he is feeling better, since you had to take care of his responsibility in the morning.

We can help our kids understand throughout the course of their childhood that a mood or emotion is not an excuse for poor behavior.

We can separate our empathy from our expectations.

If we teach our children this, we will save them from shock and betrayal in the real world. We will help them understand what others—friends, teachers, bosses, coaches, spouses—will expect of them. We will raise them to be respectful people that do not act entitled and spoiled.

If this is the standard in your family—that everyone will behave respectfully despite difficult circumstances—your home will be a more peaceful, pleasant place to be. Most of the time, nobody has more sympathy for kids than parents do. That sympathy gets in our way, though, if we use it to excuse bad behavior.

A word about compassion: If something really is genuinely awful, like the death of a beloved pet or a serious injury, for example, *that* is the time to show our kids flexibility. When we hold to our standards 99% of the time, that 1% of the time that we relax and just say "I totally understand" will have a really big impact.

6

Manners Matter

Manners are the grease that makes the wheels of human interaction run smoothly.

When my eldest was three, we were visiting family far away. They are wonderful, somewhat indulgent family who just wanted to see my son smile all the time. Every time someone would hand him a treat or toy, I would remind him to say thank you. "Oh, he doesn't need to say that," they would invariably say, with love.

It got me to thinking. These people really didn't need him to parrot back "Please" and "Thank you" every few minutes. But I do. For the next 15 years or so, it would most often be me and his father who were handing him things. We need him to ask politely because it makes us feel good, and because not everyone in the world will love him in quite the same beautiful, undemanding way as his great-grandmother.

Remember when I said that we can show empathy for our kids and still hold them to our standards? Treating others respectfully is most often demonstrated through manners.

Which "manners" are most important? One of the best parts of being the parent—you get to decide.

To get you started, here is my Top 5 list. Pick from these or just watch your family for a few days to see what is important at your house, what would grease the wheels and make it run more smoothly.

1. Please and thank you. Every. Single. Time.

2. Answer when someone speaks to you.

3. Say hello when you come in, and bye when you leave.

4. Sit up at the table.

5. If you're getting something, offer it to everyone else.

Your list might be totally different. Or you might want to make it a family project and ask each person to contribute one or two Polite Rules to put up on the fridge. You might be surprised at their suggestions. You may not even need a list, just an attitude adjustment. Be certain of one thing.

We can treat our family members well most of the time, and we should.

7

Build Respect with Every Meal

Did you ever want to be a rock star? I can't really help with that. Want to look like a rock star parent? Try this.

Most meals our kids eat are prepared by an adult. This is often a thankless job. But it shouldn't be. Teach your children to say the following three things after every single meal and they will be the most amazing guests ever, whether they are 3 years old or 17. You'll like cooking for them more, also.

1. "Thank you for lunch." To say this, your child has to figure out who cooked, get that person's attention, and say "Thank you." For younger kids it also involves figuring out which meal they just ate. My youngest has solved this huge dilemma by saying "Thank you for the meal."

2. "May I be excused?" Some families want the child to ask his own parent (even if he is at someone else's table), some families want the child to ask the host. Up to you. The trick is to have the child ask this question and wait for an answer.

3. "Where should I put my dishes?" This teaches children that homes are not restaurants. They should take responsibility for helping to clear the table.

These sentences need to each get a response before moving on to the next. Stringing them together into one incomprehensible run-on sentence really takes away the respect factor.

Practice this at home after every meal. Seriously. Every time your kiddo eats something on a plate, require these three steps. "Thank you for the ____." You're welcome. "May I be excused?" Absolutely. "Where should I put my dishes?" In the sink, thanks.

If your child is really shy, then you and she need to brainstorm. After your child has nailed this skill at your own table, the two of you can work on a solution for each of these tasks that fit her personality. For example:

1. "Thank you for the meal" can be a simple quiet "Thank you" right next to the adult the child is addressing.

2. "May I be excused?" can be directed to the child's own parent, not the host.

3. "Where should I put my dishes?" can again be a private question or the child may watch where a sibling or friend puts them and do the same. If no one else at the table is clearing, your child can simply put his dishes in the sink.

ASK DOCTOR G

Parent Q: My daughter gets invited to eat at her friends' houses. But her manners are so bad at our table, I'm afraid to let her stay. Any suggestions?

*E*ating a meal without your own parents there is such a treat for many kids. As parents, though, we often fear the impression our child will make. She might not eat most of the food (because it was *touching* another food), or she'll take four servings of pasta before other people even get firsts, or she'll talk nonstop through the whole meal. You're starting to get a picture in your head of my dinner table, aren't you? If your daughter ends her meal with the three sentences listed above, none of the rest will matter. Those parents will think she is the best behaved kid ever. My own children have used this magic on unsuspecting adults.

Once your kids have mastered this (it takes a WHILE), you can step it up if you want to. If your child has a friend over who has finished, your child can clear his guest's plate as well. If a parent has finished, he could offer to clear that plate as well. An older child can have the responsibility of clearing for a sibling too young to do it herself. As children become teenagers, they should start to learn to clear serving dishes as well. But really, this is just icing. The three sentences will make your kids a pleasure to eat with, and the most impressive pint-sized dinner guests ever!

8

Raising Good Hosts

"Can I have a friend over?" I hear this phrase a lot. After kids are about age five, letting them have a friend over can make your life a lot easier. Your child has a playmate and you get some breathing room to get a few things done. Not to mention racking up points with the friend's parents so they might invite your kiddo over in the future, giving you some actual kid-free time. As long as you can provide a safe space and some snacks, this is kind of a no-brainer.

Unless, of course, your child decides that he is going to do his own thing. Or the friend is "bored." Or the two of them fight the whole time.

So here are three suggestions for ways to make your playdate go smoothly.

1. **Come up with a plan.** Have your child come up with a list of possible activities.

   a. **Toddlers** will need your help (and supervision during the playdate).

   b. **Preschool and elementary aged kids** can write this out as a menu using words or pictures. This gives you a chance to OK the activities and gives your daughter something to do besides asking one thousand and three times when her friend is going to show up. And then the friend feels great when she is presented with a menu of choices and she gets to make all the decisions. Definitely encourage your son not to put anything on that list he doesn't feel like doing. He can even include time limits if he thinks something would get boring if they play it too long.

c. **Tweens** can make this plan in their heads, and avoid the geeky aspect of actually writing it down (too much like school, Mom).

2. **Avoid obvious trouble spots.** Please suggest that your children put away things they are not willing to share. Unfortunately, for some kids this means packing up every single one of their possessions in U-Haul boxes and moving them to a storage locker. If that describes your child, try having him call his friend and suggest beforehand a few toys or possessions that child might bring so they can each use their own. This is especially helpful for kids who love physical activity—a call to say "Hey, bring your rollerblades" makes sure everyone can have fun and that they have the same expectations about what they'll do.

3. **Manage the conflict.** So what do you do when children are fighting over a toy? A few suggestions include using a timer and taking turns, a supervised attempt at "both" using it, or a time-out for the toy. This tussling stops around age eight. Kids older than that usually argue, but don't involve parents so much. When the fighting persists or the two children have really different styles, this may be a good time to note to yourself that this kiddo only gets invited over *with* a parent.

If you're just not a "playdate" family, I'm sure this list didn't convince you to try. Remember, though, that having people over to your home is a lifelong skill our kids need to practice. Having people over is a great way to practice showing respect.

How are hosts respectful?

1. **Walk to the door to welcome guests.** The habit of coming to the door to greet a guest helps instill good manners. In addition, it gets the time together off to a good start, giving your child a chance to really notice that someone has come over rather than

continuing to watch TV or read or play. This makes guests feel special and gives your child a chance to transition. Lastly, it is much safer than yelling, "Come on in!"

2. **Give a quick tour.** "I'll put your coat over here" or "Hi! You can leave your shoes by that bench." "Let's play in my room." "The bathroom is next to the kitchen."

3. **Offer your guest whatever you're getting for yourself.** "I'm hungry—do you want a snack? I'm getting water. Would you like some?"

4. **Lastly, walk your guest to the door when he leaves.** This can be hard since, if it has been a fun visit, your child may not want to acknowledge that a friend or guest is leaving. You can point out that ending on a pleasant note will increase the chances that the guest will want to return soon.

Practice these with everyone who enters your home until they are routine. These skills will serve children well their whole lives. And someday, when you are a guest in your child's home, you'll appreciate it also.

9

Raising Good Guests

You may have noticed by now that I really like it when my kids get invited to someone else's home. This is not (just) so I can sit on the couch eating bonbons and watch The Travel Channel. Being a guest in someone's home is great life experience. When our kids go to other peoples' homes, they can learn to

1. Try new foods and activities

2. Get along with new people

3. Follow new rules

4. See the world a little differently

Our kids will grow up to be guests in the home of their boss, their coach, their fiancé's parents, and many other situations in which they will need to know how to make a good impression.

The skills we need to be a great guest take practice (I say this a lot, right?). We are more forgiving of kids than adults. So giving our kids lots of chances to try out these skills will help them be really accomplished by the time they go home with someone who really matters to them.

A friend of mine recently prepped her three-year-old for a play-date. "What will you say when you leave?" His answer: "Thanks for having me. I hope you're happy I didn't break anything!" The times we want our kids to be polite at someone else's house take some preparation.

Teach kids to show respect as a guest.

1. **Ask.** Hungry? Ask politely. See a cool toy or interesting gadget? Ask if you can play with it. Need the bathroom? Ask which one to use.

2. **Knock.** Knock on the front door when you go over, or on the bathroom door if it's closed. Don't go into anyone's (except maybe your friend's) bedroom or office. And after you knock, **wait** for an answer!

3. **Offer to help.** If you are offered something—a snack, a meal, an outing—ask, "Can I help?"

4. **Tell the truth.** If, despite your best efforts, you DO break something or spill something or flush the pet gerbil down the toilet (It happens!), speak up right away and apologize. Then go back to #3.

5. **Say thank you.** When given a ride home, a snack, or an invitation to come over in the first place, people remember the thank yous. It's a great way to get invited back.

When our kids show even some of these manners, it will help the adults around them see what good people they are. Those adults will have more patience, more compassion, and more forgiveness when things don't go well. This is the best of all reasons for good manners.

10

Titles Matter

If you live in the South, you can skip this chapter. I'd just be preaching to the choir. For everyone who was raised up North like I was, let me extol the virtues of "Sir" and "Ma'am." And don't you roll your eyes at me young lady!

Let me tell you the story of one first-grade Parent-Teacher Conference Day. Once upon a time, my husband and I went to school for conferences and heard seven different teachers sing the same song: Your Child Is Smart but He Won't Stop Misbehavin'. As we headed out of the cafeteria we were stopped by the lower school gym teacher. "Are you [insert child's name here]'s parents?" Well, lying would have been just plain wrong, so we agreed that we were. "Your son is the best behaved child in this school!" I nearly showed her a picture of this child on my phone, for clarification. "Really?" we asked. "Why do you say so?" She went on to explain that, the day before when his class came for gym, she outlined a game to play. Our darling boy raised his hand and, when called on, immediately started telling all the kids how to play it, extra rules, strategy, and all kinds of unsolicited and poorly timed information. "But when I shushed him," the teacher went on, "he turned to me, looked me straight in the eye, and said, 'Yes ma'am, I'm sorry.' I haven't been ma'amed in 10 years or more. What a good boy he is!"

Moral of the story? These two little words — "Yes, ma'am" — have a lot of power.

We want adults to respect our kids. Teaching our kids to show that extra bit of respect to adults is a great way to get them there. If your community, or own philosophy, doesn't work with "Sir" and "Ma'am," then just use titles.

Can you hear me from all the way up here on my soapbox? I know this is unusual in a lot of families. But I'm really encouraging you to stop your kids from calling adults by their first names. They can use titles with last names, like Mrs. Greene, or titles with first names like Mr. Jim and Ms. Carmen. "Coach" is good, I'm obviously a big fan of "Doctor," even "Aunt" or "Uncle" is fine. The title itself is less important than the habit of always using one.

Why am I giving you this new headache? Titles help kids.

- Adults will listen to them more.

- Titles are verbal boundaries, reminding kids to treat adults differently than peers.

- This level of respect will help get them out of trouble: "I'm sorry, officer."

- They will look forward to being an adult.

So, the next time you introduce your child to an adult, include the title.

ASK DOCTOR G

Parent Q: I'd like my children to call our neighbor Ms. Valdez, but she insists they call her Susie. What should I do?

*A*dults often unintentionally thwart parents' best efforts to teach their kids to be respectful. If you introduce your child to a grown-up and that adult brushes you off, "Oh! He can just call me Susie." try enlisting Susie's help. "We're working hard on teaching our kids to be respectful to all adults. We'd really appreciate it if he could call you Ms. Valdez or Ms. Susie."

I do know that this is unusual. But we all know that our kids can use every advantage in the world. If most kids won't be doing this, your child will only shine that much brighter.

11

Teach the Verbal Communication Secrets

Would your child agree with this sentence?

"Grown-ups are easy to impress, easy to talk to, and easy to get on your side."

If your child would laugh at that idea, you need to teach her the tricks. There is a grown-up secret code so secret most adults don't even realize they know it. However, children can crack the code with a few magic words.

You're thinking, "Magic words? Oh, my kids already know this. They say please and thank you." This is only the start! Of course these are helpful. But "Please" just opens the door. To get the grown-up to really walk through that door and help a kid out, the child has to know the rest of the code. There are three important rules to learn.

1. **Use titles of respect.** If you didn't catch Chapter 10, check it out. Even if it sounds goofy, even if nobody else does it, nothing makes a grown-up look twice at a kid (or job applicant) like one who says, "Yes ma'am" or "I will, sir." Challenge your kids to try this and see how differently adults treat them.

2. **Drop the slang.** Explain this to kids this way: I'm going to tell you something about adults that most adults don't even realize about themselves. You can make adults trust you more and understand you are a good person by USING certain words and AVOIDING certain words.

Instead of:	Say:
Yeah.	Yes!
Thanks.	Thank you!
Huh?	Excuse me?
Nuh-uh.	No, thank you.
K.	I understand.
What?!	Yes?

Using slang separates you from adults but does not impress them. Slang is friend-language only. Slang makes adults feel dumb or old and a little bit like you're making fun of them even if you're not. None of these things will make an adult take a young person more seriously.

OK, you may be thinking, "Am I teaching my kid to manipulate adults?" And I answer, "Yes, a little bit." That is the motivation you might use when talking about this to your preteen. And of course you need to do your best to get your child to use this newfound secret code for good, not evil. But the lesson is still an important one: words matter, and how you use them affects how people see you.

3. **No foul language anywhere near adults, or little kids.** Ever. No swearing, no insults, no fart jokes. Side note: Every culture has fart jokes (true story) and you may have a lovely family tradition of telling them around the dinner table, but these are for your family only. They do not impress most people. Anyway, back to the rule. Do I think good kids don't swear? No, actually. I think almost every kid swears (some more than others), but I think every kid who swears and then realizes there is an adult in the room should flinch, and apologize. Face it, when you hear a kid swear part of you thinks, "That is not a good kid." *Especially* if your small child learns a new word from that one. Even though adults curse, hearing that come out of a young person's mouth changes how we see him or her. Everyone learns the bad words at some point. The hard part to learn (as with everything) is impulse control.

So, to recap: Boundaries matter. Learning the secret code of separating the generations will help your child treat adults well and in turn be treated better by adults. The very special relationship with a trusted aunt or mentor that allows a child or teen to relax those boundaries a little is all the more special if he or she is used to treating all adults very respectfully.

12

Teach the Nonverbal Communication Secrets

It's not just what you say that makes an impression on people, it's how you say it.

Three fourth-grade boys are in the principal's office. These bright boys took it into their heads to teepee his car. At dismissal. In front of everyone. Big shocker, they got caught. Now, when the principal (who told me this story) said, "Boys, did you teepee my car?" two of them looked at the ground, shuffled their feet, and mumbled "Yeah." One stood straight, looked his principal in the eye, and said, "Yes. We're sorry." Guess which one this principal respected more after the stunt than he did before it?

Words matter, but we communicate in lots of other ways, too. I know that we are spending a lot of valuable time helping kids understand that we should not judge people by what we can see. However, we also should not pretend that adults will always look below the surface and get to know our kids before gathering an impression.

Since we know that nonverbal communication gives a lot of information, we need to teach our kids the power they have to demonstrate who they are.

1. **How they dress.** I'm all for self-expression. But, as a doctor, I believe in informed consent. What does one have to do with the other? It's like this: We dress to make a statement. There are lots

of ways to dress and lots of statements to make. Our kids need to be informed about the statements they are making with their clothes so that they can consent. Provocative, messy, sharp, goth, punk, preppy, they think about what their peers will think of their outfits. It is up to us to teach them about the impressions they will make on adults. Speaking as someone who had to be told by a store manager not to apply for a job wearing ripped jeans (sheesh, what did she care?), I can tell you that these effects are not obvious to kids.

2. **Posture**. It's a classic for a reason. Sitting up straight, standing up straight, not slouching in class or at the table, all of this matters when you're talking to a grown-up. It shows self-respect and respect for the person you are addressing. Even if it is terribly annoying to learn.

3. **Eye contact**. Kids need to practice looking people straight in the eye. For introductions, questions, apologies, even just in conversation—this is that self-respect and respect-for-others thing again. Have you ever been on a date with someone at a restaurant with TVs in the corners? Eye contact matters. Learning this also requires putting down the cell phone.

You probably have some tricks of your own to teach your kids: How to give a good handshake. The value of holding the door open for someone. The importance of standing when meeting someone new. Think of the people you know with the nicest manners (especially the teen or young adult you'd like your child to be just like) and search for the secret code.

13

Teach Your Kids to Talk to Strangers

"Don't talk to strangers" is a very confusing thing we tell kids. Why? Because we also tell them, "Say hello to the nice lady." "Say thank you to the bank teller." "Why don't you go say hi to that little boy?" We do want our kids to talk to strangers, because it's polite, and because they need to learn how.

Every adult is an opportunity for practicing manners, and learning how to get along in the world.

How many strangers do you talk to in a day? What's more, most of the time that we are addressing someone we don't know, it's because we want something from him or her: directions, information, or help. Our children need to practice seeking out, getting the attention of, and talking to adults they don't know.

First, let's address the safety issue. When you teach your young kids about stranger danger, teach them these three things:

1. Don't talk to a stranger unless you are touching an adult you know well.

2. Adults should never ask a child they don't know for help.

3. I will never send someone you don't know to get you, unless it's a police officer or firefighter in a uniform.

We can't cover every possibility, but these are good "stranger danger" guidelines to teach our children. None of these situations are likely, but it will help us to start important conversations with them, and make parents sleep better at night.

Now that we've covered the scary stuff, it's time to think about the value of strangers in a child's life. The librarian is a stranger, and so is a new coach. The manager of a store is a stranger, and also the crossing guard. But all of these folks have useful information that our child might need.

So teach kids to look at strangers as opportunities. Remind them about how to make a great first impression:

• Stand when you meet someone new.

• Look in the person's eyes.

• Use the person's name (with a title) in the first sentence, if you know it.

"Hi Coach Jackson, I have a question."

14

Seek Out Diversity

Little kids are wired to be mistrustful of people who are different from them. This protects them from wandering off with those they don't know. It helps tribes stick together, and builds relationships tighter in families. This protects young children.

It also promotes racism, sexism, and all kinds of bigotry.

No, I'm not saying that little kids are racists. I'm saying that many people have an inborn mistrust of those who are "other" or different. That mistrust does not build respect. It leads directly to disrespect.

ASK DOCTOR G

Parent Q: A dad, who described himself as a "crunchy granola liberal," was dismayed because his six-year-old wouldn't play with a child because of the color of his skin. "I always thought that the only way for kids to learn racism was to be raised by racists," this father wrote to me. "What does this mean and how can I fix it?"

Some people are innately cautious. Most young kids prefer repetition and do not like change. They want to know what to expect, and when they see something—or someone—"different" they feel lost or confused or angry. All of these reactions are understandable.

We don't teach children by what we aren't, we teach them by what we are. It's not enough to teach kids to be unbiased (as much as anyone ever can be). We need to seek out some diversity and get comfortable with it.

What color are your friends? Brown? Pale pink? Beige? Ochre? These are just words. For our kids to seek out a rainbow of friends, we need to get diversity into our lives. Religions, family structures, languages, cultures, sexuality, even Republicans and Democrats can be friends.

When children meet people from different backgrounds, they learn. They learn stories, they learn traditions, they learn respect. The problems of the world will be solved by keeping our eyes open to possibilities and new ideas. If we seek out diversity in front of and with our children, they will, too.

15

But What about Your Kids' Friends?

There's this great mom I know with three sons. Two are grown and out of the house already and one is a teenager now. Their house, in a rural area, backs up onto the township's football field. Since all of her boys have played football, this means that she has had most of the football team at her house every weekend—starting Friday night after the game—the whole fall season for the past 13 years. Her secret? In her own words: "We treat 'em the same as we treat our own kids—no better, no worse."

This means all the boys follow the same rules. Feet on the furniture is OK in the basement. Foul language is not acceptable in the house. Snacks are always available, and when the trash needs to go out she asks whichever guy is closest, blood relative or not. If they want to sleep over all are welcome, as long as they check in with their parents. But whoever is around Saturday morning is fair game for whatever project she decides needs to get done. It's amazing how fast 11 boys can clean out your garage!

What's more amazing is the connection these boys feel to this family. Even after her two older sons graduated and moved away for school and military service, their friends keep stopping by. They stop for coffee, to catch up, and never fail to ask if they can do anything to help out around the house.

There are a bunch of great reasons to expect the same behavior from your children's friends as you do from your own kids.

Reason 1: You have good rationale for most of your rules. OK, a few are arbitrary and just came out of your mouth when you were sleep-deprived and cranky; maybe they don't make any sense at all. But most make good sense and help you create and maintain the kind of home you want for your family.

Reason 2: If you expect good behavior from kids, most will rise to the occasion. They may show you very different behavior than they exhibit at home, both good and bad. Young people are very clear on the idea that different environments have different rules. For example, my kids can't eat in front of the TV for dinner, but that might be alright at a friend's house. They learn in kindergarten: the playground, the library, the classroom, and home all have different expectations. And their compliance is directly connected to how clearly those rules are enforced. What does that mean? It means kids are people, and they will try to get away with most of what they think they can get away with.

Make following your rules the price of admission for hanging out at your house.

Take the opposite approach for a second. What is the downside to letting your kids' friends be disrespectful or ignore your rules? After all, parenting your own kids is enough work, who wants to be responsible for parenting the whole world? Here is the downside: If you listen carefully you can already hear your child whining, "But it's not faaaaaiiiiiiiiiiir!" And it's deeper than that. As preteens start to look more carefully at the adults in their lives, they look first for hypocrisy. Any rules that aren't consistently enforced, or rules that apply to one person and not another, are much easier to argue with than to follow. If you require your children to be respectful but their friends can behave however they want, you are actually disrespecting your kids.

What about the child who BEGS you not to "be like that" with his friends? His sense of embarrassment is real, and so is the possible social price to be paid if you chastise a friend for swearing or enforce the sit-until-everyone-is-finished (no, I don't) or clear-your-plate rule (yes, I do). Do it anyway.

Setting aside for a minute the very important lessons to teach your child about not trying to fix everything so no one will ever be mad at her, the rules in your home are not negotiable, even with guests. So, how can you save your son or daughter the humiliation of having a strong parent? Take the blame. Every preteen agrees with one thing for sure: Parents are unreasonable. Don't make your child enforce your rules. Let your kid get in trouble a little bit with the friend so they can resent you together. As long as the behavior improves, this is a decent solution (especially if you've clued your child in beforehand, usually when he is begging you to not "be like that").

Here's an example. Your 10-year-old daughter asks if she can have Anya come over after school. Then your daughter says, "But when you pick us up don't be all … you know." You do know that she is horrified when you chastise her friends, and you decide not to torture her by making her spell it out. So you say, "The rules are the rules, kiddo. If she gets in trouble with me, do you want me to yell at you a little bit too, so your friend won't blame you?"

With this plan in place, you pick the girls up after school. Anya gets in, doesn't say hello (which you let slide), and then doesn't buckle up. You remind her and she rolls her eyes and mumbles, "I don't have to." You turn around to look at her and say, "Buckle your seatbelt, please, if you're coming with me." And then you turn to your daughter and say, "Yours better be buckled, too. I'm not willing to argue about this." In this way you've allowed your daughter to "side" with her friend without bending your rules and you've been more stern with your daughter than with her friend.

Reason 3: Teach your kids to expect respect. Hold your ground to set the example for your children. Kids may not listen to what we say, but they never fail to notice what we do. Our children will have to decide how they want to be treated as they grow. None of us want our kids to get walked on or disrespected. So don't wimp out when a guest tests you.

Reason 4: You should get to relax and enjoy your home. Letting our kids have friends over should not interfere with that. We may need to do some extra cooking or share the TV, but you get to decide how you will be treated in your home. Hold the line and you'll be happier. And you will have the pleasure of knowing more young adults that you like.

16

Your Bedroom as Your Sanctuary

My bedroom is not just a bedroom. According to my kids, it's a stash your toy chest, lounge, dining hall, and extra play space. According to me, it's sometimes the only place I can get five minutes of peace. And that is what it should be.

Your bedroom can be your sanctuary. The place that stays however you left it, where your belongings are safe from "borrowing," and you don't find any dirty-plate-surprises. It can also be a place that your children understand is special.

Parents' bedrooms are the physical representation of the adult relationship in the house, and show our kids the level of respect we want from them. We need a space that they ask to enter, don't leave their toys and stuff around, and keep conflict outside. How can we achieve this nirvana? Take these rules of conduct from the Smithsonian—those free but very well-kept museums in Washington DC.

Visitors are welcome but *may not.*

- Use loud, abusive, or otherwise improper language.
- Loiter, sleep without permission, or participate in unwarranted assemblies—which means no bringing in friends to hang out.
- Engage in disorderly conduct.
- Bring pets without permission of the management.
- Take photographs.

- Solicit for commercial or charitable purposes—no coming in to ask us for money.

- Bring in food or drink.

- Destroy, damage, or remove property.

- Climb on furniture or exhibits.

Lost-and-found rule.

- Anything left inside becomes property of the management.

    And last, but maybe most important:

- Entrance is free but visitors may only enter at certain hours of the day and with permission.

These may not all fit in your philosophy, and that is fine. But imagine your bedroom existing the way you choose. Pick the rules that make sense to you and post them. Enforce them, too.

Teaching your kids to respect other peoples' private space will help them become respectful adults. Having a protected space of your own will help you treat your kids respectfully as well.

ASK·DOCTOR G

Parent Q: My 12-year-old expects me to knock on her door and doesn't think I should go into her room unless she gives permission. This doesn't seem right but I can't explain why exactly.

Knocking on your child's door is a great way to show respect. However, you're knocking to *let her know* you're coming in, not to ask permission. Privacy is earned, and takes years to do so. How she keeps her room and what she does in her room are all part of your domain as her parent. Of course, she would like to convince you otherwise, but middle school is too young for the independence of a space that is totally unsupervised.

PART II

RESPONSIBILITY
COUNT ON IT

17

Responsibility: Building a Great Work Ethic

Responsibility means learning to be reliable, dependable, and able to meet your obligations. The ability to be responsible, coupled with the initiative to grab opportunities, is how adults achieve our dreams. Teaching our children (rather than just nagging, and arguing) to understand and meet their responsibilities will set them up to achieve *their* dreams.

As I travel the country speaking to parents, grandparents, and educators, time and again they lament to me the lack of a work ethic in our children's generation. I understand the concern, but I think what adults often forget is that very few people are born with a strong work ethic. It's not usually innate, but it can be taught.

Let me ask you a question about your child's education. Suppose that, at a parent-teacher conference, your child's teacher said, "Your daughter is great at math. I'm going to keep her doing the addition she does so well because she gets it done quickly, she doesn't make mistakes, and it would take a lot of time and individual attention for me to challenge her." How would you feel? I bet you would have a problem with that.

I know I would. We want our children's educators to keep them working at the leading edge of their ability and potential, right?

So why don't we do that at home? We could challenge our kids to do the laundry, or manage their own spending money, or clean the bathroom, or start a community service project. Instead we think that it gets done better and faster if we do it ourselves, and would take a lot of time and energy to try to get them to do that, they might not like it, or they might struggle. Consider instead:

- Once we teach a child a new skill, we can delegate that responsibility to him.

- Everything we want children to be able to do as adults we have to make sure they learn as kids.

- Every struggle is a chance to teach that work ethic.

What is a work ethic?

1. The willingness to step up to a job that needs to be done.

2. The perseverance to stick with that job until it's finished.

3. The integrity to do your best at the task (not only meet the minimum requirements).

4. The ability to put up with repetition, revision, and plain old boredom on the way to the goal.

Can you think of anything your children might want to accomplish someday that would *not* require these skills?

In this section, we're going to talk about chores, homework, sport and music practice, and lots of other opportunities for kids' work. All of these can be headaches for parents, but they are also chances: Chances to shape our kids into employees that will keep any job they manage to get. To raise entrepreneurs who beat the odds and succeed. To build adults who can support themselves and be do-gooders who can change the world.

Watch your child for a while with those four skills in mind. Does your child need help with the first challenge—recognizing that a job needs to be done by him? Or is perseverance giving him the most trouble now? Does he only do the bare minimum requested? Is it boredom that distracts him? Whichever is your child's weakness right now, you can use any of the topics in this section to overcome that challenge. You'll see a difference in the adult he or she becomes. This work may take a while to pay off, but it's worth it!

18

Relying on You

My mother was wily when I was growing up. On the bulletin board in the playroom in our house was a large smattering of truly bad art projects, done by me, along with a small poster with a poem entitled "Children Learn What They Live." I didn't especially like this poster but I sure read it a lot. It reminded me, without her ever having to say a word, to pay attention to the actions around me. Now that I'm a parent she's told me she *may* have put it up more as a reminder for herself than for me.

Have you ever seen it? It was written by Dorothy Law Nolte and includes the lines, "If children live with honesty, they learn truthfulness. If children live with fairness, they learn justice." It's quite long, but the point is immediately clear: Kids learn as much or more from what we do as from what we say.

So this next part is preachy and a little annoying. Please keep in mind that, like my mom, I'm preaching to myself more than anyone else. I need the reminder to not take the easy way out, pretend I have it all together when I don't, or let myself off the hook when I wouldn't do the same for my kids.

If children live with a good work ethic, they learn responsibility. Responsibility as an adult means making sure our family has food, shelter, clothing, and health care. Honoring commitments, doing what we say we will do, being accountable for that, and apologizing as well as fixing the situation if we don't, all mark adult behavior.

Being "responsible for" means being the cause of something. Being responsible for our kids means being the cause of much of their behavior. So this is our chance. Really it's lots of chances, every day, to teach them to be the kind of grown-ups we can be proud of someday. And, when we miss the mark, it's a chance to say so and work to do better.

So, as much as you can, do the right thing. Do what you say you will do. If you mess up, own up. Apologize and make it right as best you can. Don't hide all your mistakes from your kids, or all your struggles. Let them learn from your challenges if they can. Do your chores, finish your work, exercise, and nourish your gifts. Help your community and bring your kids along. Rather than letting this take away from your parenting time, make some of it *part* of your parenting time.

Our kids learn what they live. We can guide them by guiding ourselves. The added bonus? Our children will build faith in us. They will understand that they can count on us to tell the truth, to do our best, and to parent, even when it's hard. Because it's our responsibility.

19

Teach Kids to Get Themselves Clean

Can your child choose not to brush her teeth? Is washing his hands after using the bathroom a choice? What about bathing? Hopefully not. And yet, many of us struggle to get our kids to build these health-saving habits.

Good hygiene is a responsibility. And it's one we want to hand over to our kids as soon as possible. By kindergarten, no one is double-checking the hand-washing at school. By fourth grade, your child can get a seriously bad rep as the "stinky kid." Instead of tearing your hair out (wait, is that just me?) and nagging endlessly about these tasks, look at it as an opportunity.

We can tackle one major issue at a time, and use developmentally on-target skills to do it. Remember, building habits takes months of consistent practice (and since when are kids ever consistent?), so give yourself and your kids a break by having reasonable expectations.

Toddlers: Use the ABC trick for hand-washing.

➤ Soap and lather (water off) for as long as it takes to sing the whole song.

➤ Rinse.

Preschoolers: Follow the numbers to get bathroom jobs done.

➤ Take stick-on numbers and your child and label:

1. Toilet paper

2. Toilet flusher

3. Behind the lid (so they put it back down)

4. Soap to wash

5. Faucet to rinse

6. Towel to dry

7. Light switch

Ages 5–7: It's time to learn bath skills.

➤ Get on a schedule. Some kids resist bathing. And the medical truth is many kids do not need a bath every day. But whatever your rule is, plan it out and stick to it.

➤ He can wash all the places. He may need to be supervised to make sure it's getting done, but there is no place he can't reach to learn this skill himself.

➤ Master the shampoo. Your child is old enough to stop fighting with you about the shampoo and rinse, and learn to do it herself. If the bath is too complicated, consider "leveling up" to a shower.

➤ Toweling off is a fun moment, but make sure she can do this herself, too.

Ages 8–10: The what and why of oral health

Kids just don't prioritize brushing their teeth. It's boring. Learning to do boring things because they matter? That is part of building a good work ethic. Why is this a tween issue? Because, up until age 12, the American Dental Association says we need to be supervising our kids' brushing and flossing. Two minutes, two times a day. Seriously!

➤ Help with the "why." Get online and look at tooth decay, preferably in kids.

➤ Smell some stinky breath.

➤ Get them the tools they need in all the places they need it. Do you have a bathroom next to the kitchen? Get toothbrushes and toothpaste in there and start using them.

➤ As you start trusting kids to do this on their own, spot check their breath.

➤ Get your child to call for semi-annual dental appointments.

Ages 11–12: Manage that body odor.

Our brains are wired to help us ignore our own smell so that we can better focus on the environment around us. This fact makes it even more difficult to convince kids of their own … aroma.

➤ Deodorant does help. Most kids need this starting between ages 9 and 13. Getting it into your child's morning routine can be really frustrating, though. Trick: If your child has an object she or he picks up every morning that stays at home (comb, brush, toothpaste)—rubber band the deodorant to that object.

➤ Body spray ≠ shower. If you've ever walked into a middle school boys' locker room you will discover that many boys think rinsing off is unnecessary if only he has access to half a can of Axe Body Spray. Spray a nasty smelling sock or t-shirt and make him take a deep sniff—he'll learn otherwise.

➤ Put those laundry skills to use. Gym bags should go straight to the laundry, and your tween should be responsible for the washer/dryer/repack the bag cycle. Why would you want to touch that stuff?

These skills are crucial for maintaining good health and good friendships. Just as important, taking care of oneself is a foundation of being a responsible person.

20

Teach Kids to Get Themselves Dressed

Everybody wears clothes, so use this daily fact of life to teach your child to take great care of him- or herself. Another huge perk of teaching these tasks is that you can delegate some of the daily work with clothing to your kids. You'll teach them necessary life skills and free yourself up for more urgent issues.

Toddlers.

➤ What to wear? Two- and three-year-olds are all about the choices, right? So make sure they can only choose between items that are acceptable to you. "Do you want the blue long-sleeved shirt or the red long-sleeved shirt?" Not "What do you want to wear today?" If you go that route you'll have *that kid* in a bathing suit and rainboots trudging through the snow. And you'll definitely get *those looks* from the grandparents.

➤ Pick it up. Make sure your child knows he is responsible for getting all his clothes into the laundry basket (from wherever he drops them around your home).

➤ Toss the diaper. If your child has a wet (but not dirty) diaper, she should change it (or at least trash it) herself. This is a great first step toward potty-training.

Preschoolers.

➤ What to wear? Use your child's love for technology by checking The Weather Channel app together each morning. Use that information to encourage your child to make smart choices about clothes and outerwear for the day.

➤ Sort socks. That really annoying chore for grown-ups is just a matching game for kids. Put them to work next to you making pairs for everyone in the house.

➤ Put that folded laundry away. Once someone has folded clean clothes, your child should be able to take the neat piles and put them (almost as neatly) in the correct drawer.

Ages 5–7.

➤ What to wear? Most of us get our children's clothes without them. For the most part, that is a great time-saver. But there are some important life lessons to be found in searching for, trying on, and deciding between purchases. So sometimes … take him with you.

➤ Label that stuff. Kids lose all manner of things. I was a real "If your head wasn't attached you'd lose it" kind of elementary schooler myself. Teach kids an important step in finding lost things— practice that new name-writing skill (or sticker-peeling skill) by having them label anything they wear or take out of the house.

Ages 8–10.

➤ What to wear? Dressing up for important events—picture day, church, a performance—teaches kids to demonstrate responsibility through clothing choice. Wearing a uniform for school or games teaches responsibility as well.

➤ Sew buttons. This is a skill that comes in handy all through life, and third- to fifth-graders have the time and the talent to learn it.

➤ Time to do the laundry. Yes! Have them sort, wash, dry, and fold; all of these are within the cognitive and motor skill abilities of most kids this age. They need to learn to do it, and you don't love it so much you can't give it up, right? Keep your delicates back, though.

Ages 11–12.

➤ What to wear? Do you argue about what "fashion" is acceptable? Draw boundaries, and be willing to explain them. If your child wants you to move one of those boundaries, ask for a compelling reason why. You may not agree, but the conversation is important and will teach her valuable skills.

➤ Have a difference of opinion about hair? Tweens often want to experiment with cut and even color. Give in here if you can; it's just hair, and it grows back. Self-expression is important.

➤ Teach him to iron.

Our clothes—what we choose and how we care for them—help others form opinions about us. Whether or not that should be true, it is true. So teaching our kids how to make those opinions good ones is an important responsibility of parenting.

ASK DOCTOR G

Parent Q: My sixth-grade son wears a lot of black, "goth"-type clothes. Nothing vulgar, but he definitely gets strange looks from people when we're in public. I don't want to crush his spirit but I want him to wear something else.

Clothes are a good way for kids to express themselves. It's great that you respect your son enough to understand that this is his creativity coming out. It's also responsible to help him understand how adults will perceive him when he's dressed in a nontraditional way.

Ask him what he's noticed about others' reactions to his clothing. Solicit his feelings about those reactions. Give him some respectful feedback about what you've noticed. It's reasonable to have a certain "dress code" for your son in certain situations, like worship or school settings. Do find as many chances as you can for your son to make his own decisions about what he wears. Let him find his way through these experiences now, at an age where people will judge you more than him. You can take it!

21

Teach Kids to Get Themselves Fed

It turns out these kids want to eat every single day, and not only once. Use that very real motivation (their hunger and your desire not to cook $3 \times 7 \times 52 \times 18 = 19,656$ meals) to teach some important skills that build responsible people.

Toddlers.

➤ Clear that place. Most two- and three-year-olds eat with durable plates and cups. Take advantage of that durability to teach them how to put dishes in the sink or dishwasher.

➤ Try a new food. Want a toddler who thrives on predictability to eat something new? Give three foods: one new and two reliable stand-bys. If your little one wants seconds on the favorites, he needs to try the new food. If it's not worth it, no problem, but no seconds. No arguments, no battles. But no seconds.

➤ If you get up without asking, you're done. Getting up and coming back to the table builds some bad habits and leads to kids (and adults) eating more than we should. Teach a child that leaving the table without being excused ends the meal for that person. Every time.

Preschoolers.

➤ Don't yuck someone else's yum. Nobody likes everything, and some foods are gross to most people. But somebody worked to prepare that food, and even if I don't like it, somebody else might. We need to do the responsible thing and keep our strongly negative opinions to ourselves. It's much harder to enjoy a food after someone has "eeeeeewwwwwed" it.

➤ Use water as the go-to drink. Build that healthy habit early and teach kids to get their own drink of water whenever they feel thirsty. Put cups in an accessible place, and a cold water dispenser on a low shelf in the fridge.

➤ Eat out in a healthy way. Eating out is a treat, and one that teens and young adults enjoy as often as they can. Create responsible habits so those meals out don't cause problems later. Teach kids to:

1. Start with a vegetable-only appetizer (most kids' meals come with a veggie—ask the server to bring it as soon as you sit down).

2. Get water instead of the sweet drink.

3. Choose the sweet drink OR dessert to end the meal. Or neither.

Ages 5–7.

➤ Set the table. This chore also needs to get done almost 20,000 times, so delegate it as soon as possible. Make it easier by putting some dishes in a lower cabinet. In our house, the child who volunteers to set the table gets to choose which seat (except Mom's or Dad's) he sits in.

➤ Read a label. As kids learn to read words and numbers, teach them to practice by reading snack food labels. Knowledge is power. This way, when you say no to a junk food request, they can read why.

➤ Put away dishes. At this age, they are too young to put away the china (unless you got it from your in-laws and can't stand it), but early elementary school kids are absolutely able to sort the silverware into the drawer and put kid dishes away.

Ages 8–10.

➤ Pack a lunch. Make a list of the parts of lunch (main course, veggie, protein, side, snack, drink) and a list of each of the foods your child likes (and you can live with). Then take this chore off your list and put it on hers.

➤ Make a grocery list. This is the right age for this life lesson: Food does not magically appear in the fridge or cabinet. Ask your child to make a list of all the food he sees in the house, and post it. When he finishes something, or it's close to empty, mark it on the list.

➤ Wash some dishes. Grab a step stool and step that child up to the sink. Again, avoid the fragile stuff you love—soapy dishes slip and sinks are pretty unforgiving. He can learn to scrub the pots and pans. Seriously, if you didn't have to do that anymore, think what else you could get done.

Ages 11–12.

➤ Plan a meal. Ask your child to consider the food preferences (and any allergies) of the family and plan a nutritious dinner. If that goes well, ask for recipes. And maybe even a grocery list.

➤ Pack up the leftovers. Packing up leftovers not only teaches that ever-important skill of eying up containers to see how much will fit, but it also requires learning about food safety. What needs to be refrigerated? Frozen?

➤ Soda is dessert. Check out the calories in a can of soda. It's equivalent to eating 9.5 sugar cubes. As a family doctor, I'd rather you avoided soda entirely in this age group; however, if it's a part of your tween's life, teach her to see it as ice cream or cake, and not a drink to go with a meal.

What we eat matters. How we choose it, acquire it, prepare it, and clean it up is also important. Teaching our kids these lessons will help them be healthier and more responsible about their health. Remember, the best possible way to teach kids how, what, and when to eat, and how to manage the before and after, is to eat dinner as a family just as often as you can. It really is as powerful and good for your kids as you've heard.

22

Teach Kids to Get Themselves Fit

Kids are wired to be active. After all, don't we spend the first several years of their lives trying to get them to sit still for a minute? But that motivation to move can get squashed by circumstances. Schedules, screens, and society can all conspire to suck that drive to sweat right out of them. How can we raise our kids to love activity and seek out physical fitness for themselves? By starting young, being consistent, and praising activity rather than thinness. Also important (and this is the worst part) is being active ourselves.

Toddlers.

➢ Exercise in front of them. Don't wait until nap time every time you work out (you'll do it a lot less if you only exercise when they're down—trust me!).

➢ Add exercise to household tasks, like clean up. Put on some music, as it makes boring tasks go faster, brings smiles, and encourages booty-jiggling.

➢ Bust boredom with movement. When your child is getting antsy or waiting for something, teach her the habit of turning to exercise as a great answer.

Preschoolers.

➢ Involve your children in your own exercise. In addition to throwing them in the stroller or bike seat, get your kids dancing to the video, biking while you run, and doing jumping jacks next to your workout machine.

➢ Teach her to swim. This is a life-saving skill. Don't put it off.

➢ Use physical exertion to improve his mood. Does your child realize that sweat burns off frustration, sadness, and anger? Let him learn this life lesson.

Ages 5–7.

➢ Brag about your exercise. If you're fitting exercise into your alone time, make sure your child knows you do, and why you value that.

➢ Teach her to ride a bike. Independence, perseverance, and fitness all come from bike-riding.

➢ Encourage her to be active with her friends. This is about the age when girls start to sit down for more of their play. Remind her of the fun of tag, hide-and-seek, and soccer.

Ages 8–10.

➢ Challenge each other to exercise. Get yourself and your child a pedometer and see who can walk the most steps this week. Whoever wins gets to pick an outdoor activity to do together this weekend!

➢ Walk a dog. If you don't have one, see if there is one in the neighborhood that could use some extra exercise. This teaches responsibility toward animals and the habit of helping a neighbor while showing your child what fun it can be to walk.

➢ Make exercise a good option to get out negative feelings. Add music for a big boost. At our house we got a kid-sized punching bag. Our sons are never allowed to hit each other in anger, but can go punch the heck out of that bag, do jumping jacks, or run: whatever exercise works to burn off tough emotions.

Ages 11–12.

➤ Ask to learn a kind of exercise. Challenge your tween to find a new kind of exercise that inspires her. Then learn it together.

➤ Do some outdoor work for your family or for a neighbor. Cleaning up a yard, shoveling snow, and sweeping the sidewalk provide lots of outdoor opportunities to get some chores done and be active.

➤ Talk about body image. I know parents worry that bringing up BMI, thinness, fatness, anything-ness about weight could cause problems with tweens. However, these thoughts and conversations are part of middle schoolers' lives. Instead of leaving them to make all their own judgments and decisions, get in on the conversation. Ask questions, listen to their thoughts and opinions, and find out what worries them and how they see themselves. Only then can you help.

When kids learn to participate in physical activity, to value it and seek it out, they are more likely to keep doing it. The human body was built to move and do physical work. Most people who exercise are active in other areas of their lives as well. An active life will lead our kids to a productive life.

23

Chores: Good for You *and* Them

Sounds preachy, right? But seriously, this chapter is all good news. This chapter is about making your life easier. Hang in with me for a minute, you'll see what I mean. First, a story to explain my perspective.

One day I was (figuratively) smacked upside the head by a five-year-old boy. He and his mom and I were talking at his well-child checkup. This boy was growing well, a little short for his age and a little skinny, but well within the range of normal. We talked about all the usual stuff—sleep (11 hours), nutrition (good), screen time (a few hours a week), and safety. He didn't have a bike, but he assured me that he wore a helmet whenever he got to ride a horse. This was a rural community and his parents managed a small farm. "How often do you ride?" I asked. "Every day, if I finish my chores early enough." "What chores do you do?" Well, let me tell you, this was a long list. He watered and fed all the animals, emptied the trash in the barn, gathered eggs, and swept the barn. He did this every morning before getting on the school bus for kindergarten.

I had only been working in this area for a few months, but this turned out to be fairly typical of the responsibilities of an early elementary school child in this county. Not in 1898, mind you, in 2002. I would be willing to bet that my kids wish I had never learned this particular lesson.

So kids *can* do a lot to help with house and family work. Which brings us to the question: How much *should* they do? This is a deep, philosophical question. So I'm going to tell you why I think chores are an awesome idea. You are going to decide if this makes sense for you and your family, and how much is enough—or too much. Overall, I think parents like the idea of having their kids do chores, for lots of good reasons. I do get questions about this and concerns as well. So, questions first.

Why? Chores, responsibilities, jobs, opportunities, marshmallows— it doesn't matter what you call them as long as children do them. Chores teach children how a family works day to day. Doing chores protects them (and you) from the entitled attitude that everyone around them should make things happen for them without their own work. Most importantly, chores make kids even more a part of the family. Each of us feels more invested in something when we have done some work.

When your family enjoys a good dinner, it is important that they appreciate the chores that went into that. Meal planning, grocery shopping, putting food away, cooking, cleaning up after cooking, table setting, serving, clearing the table, washing the dishes, putting them away, and packing up leftovers—Wow! Thanks for dinner. Hearing a list of chores is not the same as doing that list. This has the added benefits of making your kids really appreciate going out to dinner on occasion and helping the cook in the family feel less like a martyr. Seriously, these people want to eat several times a day, every single day!

Who? Everyone old enough to walk is old enough to have some responsibilities. Toddlers love to help, and will be proud to see that they can. At the other end of the age spectrum, busy teens should not be exempt from chores. Doing the mundane for your tweens teaches them a sense of entitlement that will not serve them well when they are looking for a job (or a mate).

What? Every single thing you want your kids to be able to do for themselves as adults they can learn while they are still at home. Start with the things you like to do the least. Not only will this (eventually) get you out of doing these things yourself, but you will be more patient with your children's mistakes while they learn. A 10-year-old can pack lunch for himself and his siblings. A seven-year-old can learn to do and fold laundry. A five-year-old can feed the dog or cat, and take out the recycling to the garbage can (the garbage may be too heavy and harder to clean up if it spills). Get some help bringing in the groceries and putting them away. Ironing probably has to wait for the tween years, as does washing or drying good dishes. Although I would be willing to live with fewer place settings to get out of cleaning the kitchen, maybe that's just me. You get the idea, right? Everything that needs to be done to make your home run smoothly are skills you should teach your kids.

One other thought about the "what." Make sure that some of the jobs you give your child benefit someone else in the house. It's important to hang up your own jacket, clear your own plate, and toss your own clothes in the laundry basket. It's also important to do chores that help others in the house. Clear your plate *and* your baby brother's, or gather up the garbage from all the cans in the house. Straighten a room that others messed up, too. Chores teach personal responsibility but also good family citizenship. Remember, after some practice, chores should make your life easier. This frees you up to do what your children can't do—parent!

When? Every day. Chores are just grease to make life's wheels run more smoothly. You do some every day, and your kids can, too. These can take just five minutes, or lots longer, depending on the work and the child. A big chore (like laundry) might be once a week, but smaller things like setting the table for dinner or feeding the iguana or emptying the dishwasher can happen each day. Some families use a chore chart, some have a list, and some have a running assignment so it doesn't have to be written down. Figure out what works for you and your family. Do you keep a to-do list? Then teach your kids to do that. Do you take care of things on the fly? Fine. Include your family in the getting-it-done-when-you-think-of-it plan.

Where? Everywhere. OK, mostly chores happen at home. Everywhere you have responsibilities as a family your kids can have some responsibilities, too. If you are on vacation in someone else's home, teach your kids the good manners of straightening up before you leave. Don't just show them that you pitch in to help cook or clean or make the beds, give them some jobs also. This lessens your work and makes them better guests. You'll get invited back more. When they are at a friend's house, make sure they know that you expect them to be helpful. If someone is carrying in groceries, they should offer to help. If the garbage is full, offer to take it out. Point out to your children that this is a great way to be asked over again. As we talked about in the "Respect" section, when your child has a friend over, get him to help out. You will get an extra set of hands, and most people like to feel included, even in work.

How? Hardest question last. And really this is two questions: How can you figure out what your kids can do? And how can you get them to do it?

Give up some control. Your children will *not* do these jobs as well as you would. The clothes will have some wrinkles, the table will not be as clean, the bathroom will not sparkle. Kids do not notice dust under things, and, if they do, they will pull the object forward a little so you don't see the dust. But they will be learning that things do not clean themselves, and how to clean. Don't you want your little future-employees and future-spouses to know that? If there is a chore that has to be done very well so that you can be comfortable, keep that one for yourself. Actively search for the jobs that can be done imperfectly.

You will have to supervise, oversee, and sometimes do something again. Especially at first and especially with younger kids, these chores will take far more time than if you did it yourself. If you are all about efficiency, think of this as a time investment. Things that take twice as long now will be things that you can stop doing entirely in the future. Here's a great example. If your daughter has shoes with laces, you could tie them for her every day. Or you could take time to teach her how to tie them, retie them a bunch of times, encourage her, and check them until that happy day when you can just say "Go put on your shoes" while you get your keys and to-go cup and run the dishwasher. Then you're both ready to go at the same time.

How do you get kids to do chores? Again, we're going to talk all about getting kids to respond to you the way you would like in the last section. But let's talk about the basics of this situation.

Toddlers can think of anything as a game and they spend all their awake time imitating. Capitalize on that and let them.

➤ Wipe the table and then give him a sponge for the high chair tray.

➤ Put your dish in the sink and then let her put hers in.

➤ Play "concentration" with the shoe pile by the front door.

➤ Hang coat hooks lower so he can hang up his jacket when you hang up yours.

Elementary school kids are making all kinds of transitions and always looking for ways to be more grown-up. So this is part of that new territory.

➤ Make some of these things a privilege. "You are now old enough to be trusted with the vacuum cleaner. Be careful of the dog...."

➤ If you think your children will see through this, then connect chores to goals your kids already have. People this age are old enough to understand the linking of privileges and responsibilities. When our eldest turned seven, we told him we had some news: he was old enough to have his own e-mail account (fully supervised) and old enough that he needed to do our family's laundry once a week. Each of the boys who've turned seven at our house have gone through this learning experience and very few of our clothes are now pink or tiny.

Middle schoolers are at a different stage. They are peer-focused, self-involved, and usually pulling away from the family, at least for a few years during this time. If you have never required your children to help around the house day-to-day, they will resist this with incredible strength. If you decide this is a worthy change to undertake, be prepared for resistance and have your strategies in mind.

➤ Look first at the "contract" concept in the Responsiveness section, and lay out these expectations and the advantages and consequences clearly. You may consider, when making a list (and start with a short one) of chores you want your teen to do, making a list of all the chores you do for them.

Chores teach good lessons. Children learn to contribute and expect things from themselves in addition to those around them. And many hands make light work. Lighter work for you means more time to enjoy your family, and better parenting.

ASK DOCTOR G

Parent Q: Should we pay our kids to do chores?

Some families do, and I see the lessons to be learned from that. We decided not to link getting allowance to doing chores for a couple of reasons. The main reason we give our children for having to do their chores is that it's part of being in a family. Everyone pitches in to the level that he can (not to the level that he wants to). This is not something we pay for, it's something that we are all obligated to do and all benefit from. My husband pointed out that paying our boys to do chores made it like a job. And you can quit a job! We did not want to face the day when a child decided he'd rather skip allowance than do what he'd been asked to do. The upshot is, if we're on vacation and you don't end up having to do your usual chores that week, you still get your allowance. And if you are in trouble for some reason and part of your punishment is no allowance, you still have to do your chores!

However, if there is a big parent-initiated project, like the yard sale I took it into my head to have this past summer, and you want a lot of help from your kids, you might choose to pay for excellent help. And if you are asking your tween to do something you regularly pay someone else to do, like be a parent helper, talk to your older child about what the responsibility entails and what you are willing to pay for a job well done.

24

Homework: It's Magic!

Some day your child is going to have a job. This may be in just a few years or it may be a decade or more in the future. Let's imagine that, even if she doesn't love this future job, she would like to keep it for a while.

In the competitive workplace, keeping a job isn't easy. But it is simple. To keep your job, you have to provide a product or service for a customer. This product or service has to be what the customer wants, when the customer wants it. Some of you are trying to punch holes in my simplistic theory, right? What if my child is an Olympic athlete, a diplomat, a dancer? Think about it, though: If they are (heaven willing) earning a paycheck at any job, something must be done regularly, on time and within certain specifications.

Want the magic formula for keeping your future-adult child from getting fired? Homework!

Now the skeptical readers are getting all fired up (little pun). Homework? What is this woman talking about? Most jobs don't have homework. And very few jobs require long division that shows your work, or a diorama about wigwams or rock formation. All true. But all jobs require some product or service on time that meets certain requirements.

Doing homework is your chance to make sure that your children have the skills they need to be great employees or successful entrepreneurs. In fact, it may be your only chance to help them learn the skills they will need to succeed at *any* job they get. Doing homework teaches some math, some reading, some other school-oriented skills that are important this week or this year. Better than that, though, homework teaches how to get tasks done on time, the way the customer wants it.

Imagine that your child is the employee, given the task of creating a product for a client or customer, and the teacher is the customer. One customer says, "I need a box with an artistic representation of the woodworking industry in Pennsylvania. I need it next Friday." Another customer says, "I require one page from the math workbook completed and delivered each morning." The next customer places a standing order for the employee to have a new list of words memorized for meaning and spelling every week. A fourth customer wants a paragraph written in Spanish in a journal every other day with occasional more intensive projects. The last regular customer needs an entire social studies textbook to be read over the course of three months with two tests on content during that time.

Let's face it, parents struggle with homework, or just hate it altogether. How to help, when to intervene, when to back off.... So what is your role? You're the project manager. It isn't your job to *do* any of these jobs, but it *is* your job to make sure that they're all on track to get done. You help the employee set up a timeline and figure out about how long each project takes. You can recommend guidelines (maybe only one sport per season or a limit of two after school activities). You can identify scheduling conflicts (out of town trip or frequent play practice as a performance gets closer). You can provide resources (school supplies, tutoring, rides to the library, double shot espresso—kidding).

You can't do these projects yourself. You don't have time, you probably have other employees to manage, and you have your own "customers" to satisfy. And, hello, you did this already! You memorized the vocabulary, you learned that if you glue a project while on the bus to school it will fall apart on the way to class before it has a chance to dry, and you found out that teachers know when you got someone else to basically do your homework for you or didn't study for the quiz.

It's good that you learned all that stuff. Don't get in the way of your children learning all of it themselves. Your children's teachers want them to learn the math or the vocabulary. You need them to learn the life skill of managing work.

What does this mean in the homework trenches? Look at the usual problems. One night, too much work? It is a great idea to help your child prioritize. The spelling test is most important because it's a larger portion of the grade than the daily math work. Daily math work will definitely get checked, but Spanish journal might not, so your child could do two paragraphs tomorrow night. One subject taking waaaaay longer than expected? Teach the skill of flexibility. Set it aside and do the other stuff, then come back. Taking a break from the homework may make it less frustrating (at least for you), and it might be easier knowing there is nothing else to do afterward.

ASK DOCTOR G

Parent Q: My child routinely gets ready for bed and then suddenly remembers a homework assignment. Last night it was a poster about rocks. Should I help so it gets done faster? She needs sleep.

*T*his is an important decision. You could shuffle all the other projects off your own list to dedicate hours to helping your child do something at the last minute. This might be the right thing to do once if your daughter is usually incredibly responsible. Keep that bigger life lesson in mind, though. She might need to learn consequences more than she needs to learn about rock formations. You could suggest that she do as much as possible before school in the morning and then tell the teacher her poster will be fantastic but late. Sleep is important, and her teacher will give her an important lesson in using and checking her assignment notebook more diligently.

When your employee throws you a curve ball and you don't know what to do, picture the future. Imagine the tough but fair boss you want to prepare your child for. What does that boss expect? What skill gets your child a good review? What attitude gets him fired?

This analogy isn't perfect. First of all, your child can't be fired. But there are negative consequences to not getting the work done. And there are performance reviews (tests and report cards) to give him a sense of how he's doing. Learning from those reviews (not just suffering through them or hiding them in the bottom of a backpack) is an important skill also. School is about learning how to work.

Here is the best part. It doesn't matter if your children are *terrible* at the schoolwork they are working on, they are still learning the life skills they will need to keep a job. Grades can only improve from a good work ethic and responsible behavior.

I skated through this whole chapter without addressing the arguments we can have with our kids about homework. That's because *my* children *never* argue. Ouch! Those lightning bolts hurt. OK, seriously, all kids whine about homework and employees who whine about work don't last long in their jobs. We're going to deal with this (the arguments *and* the whining) in the last section. So I hope you keep reading....

25

Practice, Practice, Practice: The Perks and the Pitfalls

A few months ago I raised my hand to knock on an exam room door and go in when I overhead an exasperated conversation. A dad and his 11-year-old were arguing about their after-the-doctor plans. In a tone of voice that made it clear he'd said this 143 times before, the son said, "But I don't WANT to practice the clarinet! I don't even LIKE band anymore!" The dad answered, "Well then don't think of it as practicing the clarinet. Think of it as practicing … practicing!" I walked in during the dumbfounded silence that followed Dad's premise.

Practice is the opportunity to learn from your hobbies. Did you take lessons as a kid? Piano or Sunday School or swimming, gymnastics or soccer or dance, the point is not to create a star. Rather, the point is to have fun, learn some skills, and sneak in some life lessons along the way.

The perks.

1. **Fun!** Hobbies should be fun. Activities are a time to let our kids guide the curriculum. For the most part, they get to pick what they try and which friends they want to be with in a group activity. The more fun the activity, the easier it is to sneak in the life lessons.

a. Now, maybe you've decided that your child needs to take lessons for something that he doesn't enjoy. That can be valid. If so, make clear short- and long-term goals and tell your child about them. What if your child is having trouble with math? The teacher has told you about all the research showing that kids who can read music improve in math. So you decide on piano lessons. Tell your daughter why you're doing this! "I DO know you're not interested in piano. But you've been frustrated by math and this will make math easier. So, practicing piano can replace some of your math time. Once you've learned to read music we can decide together if you'll stop piano lessons." Then find a piano teacher who gets the math-music connection, and is at least a little bit fun.

2. **Learn some skills.** Think of all the great life lessons your kids can get without you ever having to tell them in words:

- Develop athleticism even if you're not going to be a professional athlete.
- Understand the arts better despite the fact that you may not be an artist.
- Gain some confidence, work as a team, or learn to do something alone.
- Work with a coach or a teacher that shares a passion with you.

All these are valuable even if your child engages in this activity for only a few months. Think back on a lesson you or your partner took as a kid. Do you still do that thing? Even if you don't (and you probably don't), chances are good you took something from that experience that has been an advantage later on.

3. **Life skills** are the biggest perk of hobbies that involve practice of any kind. There is career advice that goes like this: "Do what you love and you'll never work a day in your life." This is the chance for your child to learn that "work" can be fun and that sometimes even fun stuff takes work. Here is your child's chance to practice practicing.

ASK DOCTOR G

Parent Q: My son was so excited to start basketball with his friends. Now that he has gone twice he is no longer interested. Should I make him go or let him quit?

Y*ou* know the value of sticking with something until a natural endpoint, whether it's the end of the class or the end of the season or after a recital of some kind. Quitting something can be the right thing to do, if it's not the norm for your child. There is an important lesson to be learned from stopping something that is painful or damaging in some way. That lesson can be learned once or twice. But keep in mind the example sticking with something can teach your son about commitments. Learning to be dependable is probably more important than whatever reason basketball didn't live up to his expectations. You need to look at your son and decide if, this time, he needs the lessons he will learn from your flexibility and compassion or the lessons he will learn from perseverance.

The Pitfalls.

1. **After school activities do not have superpowers.** They can't change who your child fundamentally is. Sports can't make your child an athlete if she isn't, drama class won't make your child a TV star, and Cub Scouts isn't going to turn your child into an outdoorsman if he only likes to sleep in his own bed.

2. **Don't live vicariously through your kids' activities and achievements.** Teams and lessons can suck parents into this mindset: "I always wished I had taken martial arts so my child must do this." Give your children some autonomy about what they choose and how serious they are about it.

3. **Let's talk about limits.** Do not try to create the Renaissance child in one semester. The kid that is on three teams, plays two musical instruments, takes lessons in another language, and then goes home to feed his partridge in a pear tree may also need to fit in time for serious psychotherapy. In our house we go by the "you pick one and we pick one" philosophy. For our younger kids, this has meant that they pick one activity and we pick swimming. Once they are proficient in the water, we reevaluate the second activity. We have rarely allowed a third activity, and only when two or more kids can attend the exact same lesson. That way we sneak in some brother bonding time along with the lesson. Do what works for your family. This means doing what actually works for everyone, not what you wish would work!

Sum it up? Get your child to pick something fun to do that takes practice. Then make sure she practices. When that activity peters out, pick something new. The rest of it will follow.

26

Money, Money, Money, Money: Allowance

A crucial responsibility is the ability to handle money. How much to spend, when to buy things, when to pine for them, how to get more money, and how to divvy it up are important skills for thriving in adulthood. Would you prefer your children learned these skills starting at age 5 or age 35? I say let's start before they have a credit score.

OK, first of all, if we want our kids to learn about money they have to get some. This usually means allowance. Once kids are old enough to understand the comparative values of each coin and each bill, it is a good time to start allowance. In our house, that means sometime in first grade, since that is when our school's math curriculum teaches money.

Allowance is *not*

- **Payment for chores.** If we're on vacation and a child doesn't have to make school lunches (oh yes, we do make them do that), he still gets allowance. If he is grounded from allowance, he still has to do chores.

- **"Mine and I can do what I want with it."** Parents still get final say over purchases, thus controlling intake of candy, plastic junk made in China, and scary video games.

- **All spending money.**

Allowance is a teaching tool. First figure out what you want to teach, THEN figure out how much you want (and can afford) to give. Every week our kids have to divvy up allowance. Ten percent goes to "Donate." This is money they can give for school fundraisers, or to whatever worthwhile cause appeals to them. The rest is broken up in even thirds. One third in "Spend" can be used for (agreed upon) spur-of-the-moment purchases. One third in "Save" can be used only for planned goals. The last third in "Invest" is literally to invest.

- **Donating is power.** Here you can give your child that most precious gift: total autonomy. She may donate this money to any cause that accepts donations (note that I did NOT say older siblings or neighbor kids, I said "cause." If your daughter is interested in saving the Pygmy Platypus in Argentina, she can send her money there. If he is concerned about the homeless person close to his bus stop, he can go with you to the grocery store and pick up a gift card to give to that person with his money. My husband and I (like many great employers) give a 1:1 matching gift to any charity our children choose to support.

- **Spending is freedom.** The freedom of spending money is sweet. Freedom for kids to use this grown-up currency and practice grown-up skills. The freedom for parents to stop having to consider every spur-of-the-moment purchase request their kids toss at them. "Can I *please* get that brightly colored cheaply made replica of a character on a TV show I watched once that I will lose or break in 2.8 seconds?" Well, sure honey, buy it yourself if you have enough money in "Spend" and then you can learn from the experience and I don't need to be frustrated when you lose it or it breaks.

- **Spending is prioritizing.** There is a shift in priorities that children experience when the money that goes out comes from their own piggy bank. Even six- and seven-year-olds can learn early budgeting when they know the school donut sale is only available to them if they keep at least one dollar of spending money until Friday.

- **Spending is a learning experience.** No matter your child's age (now or later), everyone uses a little spending money. Whether it's for Starbucks or the video arcade or an impulse buy during weekly grocery shopping, learning joy and exercising moderation in spending are important lifelong skills.

- **Save for what matters.** What is worth saving for? That is completely up to you. This is where you start to teach your kids how your own morals and ethics play out in your purchasing decisions. When your precious child says, "Can I save up for that Smash Crash Blaster?" you have the opportunity to talk about what you feel is or isn't a worthwhile purchase. This is different than "Spend" because the money is more significant. This is only to point out that, though the money may be "his," the responsibility is still yours. Don't let your kiddo save up for something you don't endorse.

- **Saving takes patience.** Take this opportunity to teach delayed gratification. The longer she saves for the Lego set, the bigger the set she can buy. "Spend" can always be added to "Save," but not the other way around. The money in "Save" should not be used on impulse. If there is a big purchase that your son one day decides he wants, he needs to wait a week or so to see if it is still so important.

- **Saving is learning, too.** The lifelong skills to be learned here are many. Keeping back a third of each paycheck in high school (jobs are the next chapter) for big purchases, even if you don't yet know what those purchases are, is a crucial lesson. Let's not underestimate the resilience of having cash in the bank for unexpected events.

- **Invest in yourself.** I sound like a bank commercial, don't I? The future is an expensive place. This money can be saved up for a mode of transportation (bike, car) or education or a place to live or perhaps a once-in-a-lifetime trip. But "Invest" means it goes someplace for more than a year. Savings accounts are great, but kind of quaint given today's interest rates. I recommend looking online for reputable banks that give CDs (Certificates of Deposit) with no minimum balance. Then every so often (about every 6 months works), you can open one (in your child's name) that has a decent interest rate.

- **Invest in learning.** This is a chance to learn about interest rates, banks, and planning. Most adults (myself included) feel shaky here, and stressed, so we put off talking to our kids about these choices. Go to your local bank and ask the manager who will sit down with you and your children (even elementary school kids) and explain these issues. This is seriously responsible.

I know I haven't told you how much money to give them. Sorry, you're going to have to duke that out with your own bank account. Remember, there are 52 weeks each year, times however many kids you have, a certain rate of increase and about 12 more years if you start in first grade. Maybe start small?

These guidelines can apply to all the money that comes to our kids, from odd jobs, birthdays, grandparents, gambling ... OK, just making sure you were paying attention. Gambling is *not* a good idea for kids. When our sons get or earn money from someone else, they still need to divide it up according to our guidelines, because we're the parents and we say so.

Money is a crucial parenting tool. The more we teach our kids about this when we are the "employers," the better they will manage their own money as adults and the less they will need to ask from us later. Truthfully, this is an opportunity to ready our children for their journey, all the while increasing their respect for work and giving them the skills to be responsible.

27

Technology: Make It a Force for Good

Do you feel like apps and phones and games and videos make it easier or harder to be an effective parent?

Technology is here to stay. I for one am pretty thrilled with technology. As parents, though, we often have worries about tech and screens. Are they poisoning our kids? Are we relying on them too much? Are we changing the fabric of our culture by plugging in preschoolers and letting tweens live online?

I get a lot of comfort from the fact that our parents had these same worries about TV. Their parents voiced these same concerns about rock 'n' roll. And *their* parents worried about kids who sat by the radio to listen to the trashy variety shows in the evenings. We all look at the new developments entering kids' lives and wonder "What are we doing?!"

Technology is a tool. Like any tool, its worth is controlled by how we use it. The analogy that helps me make (fairly) consistent decisions about what my kids do online is to think of their tech use like I think about their food. I want them to eat, but I want them to eat mostly healthy foods, with just a little junk food for fun and variety. Also, I don't want them to spend *all* their time eating, no matter how healthy the meals and snacks are.

If you accept that media and technology will be a part of your child's life, then use it as a tool that helps you teach the lessons and get the behavior you want! The way we approach watching, playing on, and using screens can teach our kids responsible behavior both online and off.

Toddlers.

➤ Start to teach balance by making sure that time in front of a screen is only one of many ways your little one spends his play time.

➤ Use technology the way you use books—a little time alone with one is fine, but just as kids might begin to tear or chew on a book, they are likely to use devices in destructive ways if they get too much time by themselves. Sit together and watch a show or play a game. This reinforces your child's learning, strengthens your family bonds, and lessens any guilt you have about plugging in.

➤ Screen nutrition: Kids this age can spend *all* of their limited online time with educational games and apps and shows—it is entertaining them at the same time.

Preschoolers.

➤ Teach balance for health. Let your kids "earn" some of their screen play through exercise. Use music videos or dancing games to inspire movement, or just trade them. An hour of running around time balances out half an hour of screen time.

➤ Kids this age learn even more when they co-view or watch with an adult who is reinforcing the activities or lessons on the screen. Help kids see screens as a path to education that happens to be entertaining.

➤ Self-monitoring is an important responsibility. If you have time limits for screen play, get your child a timer. She can play for 20 minutes today, but needs to stop on her own when the timer goes off. If she can remember to do that consistently, she can earn a slightly longer time.

➤ Screen nutrition: Talk about online content in terms of food. Give more time to "broccoli" games and apps than to "junk food" games, and make sure your child starts to understand the difference.

Ages 5–7.

➤ Demonstrate balance through your own online life. Recently I asked a parent in the office what work he does. Before he could answer, my seven-year-old patient told me, "He plays video games all day!" This turns out not to be the case—the dad says he hardly ever gets to play games—but that is how his son interpreted all his time with the computer. Talk to kids about what you do with your tech time, and help them see that you also only "play" a small percentage of the time.

➤ Talk about content. Kids this age may begin to navigate around without you. Even while you keep an eye on their behavior, let them know that you want to hear from your children if they stumble on something new, scary, or weird.

➤ Screen nutrition: Ask your child to start to rate media himself. On a scale of broccoli to ice cream sundae, how "nutritious" is what he wants to do?

Ages 8–10.

➤ Balance has to include time your child is not with you, as this is a skill we're trying to teach kids for their own lives. When your daughter goes to a friend's house, ask her to look for some variety—how much time she spends with a screen compared to playing a board game, listening to music, or hanging out without a screen.

➤ Privacy takes responsibility. We have to talk to our kids about the genuine dangers of sharing too much information online. Give kids enough information so that they will take this seriously; that doesn't mean you need to tell them everything. Then give them clear guidelines about when to check with a grown-up:

- Before sharing their age, birthday, last name, address, or school.
- Before joining a website that requires e-mail or other personal info.
- When creating an avatar or account on any site.
- When chatting in any online community or with anyone they don't know in person.
- Before changing a password—every password has to be written down where a parent can find it.

➢ Start talking about cyber-bullying. Watch some videos about this together, talk about who your child is online, and identify the clear connection to who she is in real life. Help kids be responsible for how they treat others, and hold others accountable for treating them well, too.

➢ Screen nutrition: Challenge your kids to find content they like presented in a healthy way. As kids become more Internet savvy, hold them accountable for what they watch, not just how much. As they show responsibility, they can build your trust and earn a little bit more independence.

Ages 11–12.

➢ Balance for tweens is about demonstrating priorities. Teach your child the values your family places on academics, health, and fun by helping your tween give time to each area that represents those values. Tweens have returned to the now-now-now gratification they wanted as toddlers; help them (again) learn to put off the fun until the more important stuff is handled.

➢ Give devices a bedtime. Your child doesn't have a cell phone, *you* have a cell phone (or tablet or MP3 player) that you let that child use, even if the device was a gift from someone else. So devices have to "go to bed" a half hour before your child does—on the charger in *your* bedroom.

➢ Middle schoolers want cell phones. Use that carrot to build great responsibility:

- Connect keeping track of all belongings to getting a cell phone.
- Hold them accountable for tech rules on all devices.

- Ask your child for a list of cell phone rules.
- Require a small rental fee each month to keep the phone.
- Sign all of these like a contract (just like the ones we have to sign to get the phone from our carrier) and take the phone back if the contract is broken.

➤ Screen nutrition: Just as middle schoolers suddenly have access to a lot of junk food to eat, they also get introduced to tons of online "junk food." Let them continue to build your trust by making good choices or talking to you when they don't, but keep checking up on them. And when your child says, "You don't trust me!" you can tell him "I trust you ... to be 12."

Technology is about tools, specifically the tools our kids want. Using that technology as a tool that will build our child's character gives us peace of mind and puts our child on the path to being an adult we will really enjoy and admire.

28

Forms: Don't Fill 'Em out!

Life has forms. I think kids' forms are the biggest pile. Instead of being stressed by your elementary or middle schooler's forms, don't fill them out. Instead, use this as an excellent opportunity to teach your child the skill of completing questionnaires, permission slips, health histories ... everything.

Why should you pass over this time-honored parent tradition to your children?

1. They will build many important skills from filling out forms.

2. These are forms for things kids want or need to do. Get them invested in the process.

3. If you delegate some of this work, you have plenty of other important things to do that your kids can't help with, right?

Preschool.

➤ Show your children the forms and ask them some of the questions. "Last name?" "Birthday?" "Mother's name?" "Her cell phone number?" "Allergies?" This will encourage your children to start memorizing basic, important information and taking responsibility for their own facts. And yes, your preschooler should have your cell phone number memorized—this is a crucial piece of information!

K–second grade.

➤ As soon as your child can read, ask her to read the questions to you.

➤ When her writing becomes legible, ask her to fill out her first and last name, along with your phone number.

➤ Once she's mastered that, give each field trip, picture day, and permission slip to your child with the instructions to read the whole thing, and fill out what she is sure of, bringing it back to you to finish together and for you to sign.

Third–fifth grade.

➤ Children this age are ready to learn that the things they want to do, like sports participation, camp, after school activities, or youth group, all have forms, too. Make the forms part of their homework, not yours. Offer to help with anything confusing, and go over the forms together before you sign and write the check.

Middle school.

➤ In addition to beginning-of-the-school-year forms and all the ones I've mentioned, middle schoolers should expect to fill out applications on their own. Talk to your tweens about filling out online forms, and checking in with you about the security of this each time.

➤ Going to the doctor's office? The receptionist will hand you a form to fill out about your child's health history. Give it to your child. Whatever he doesn't know, it is time he learned.

What will our kids learn by filling out forms?

• Reading and writing skills
• Scheduling and planning
• Thoroughness and persistence
• Follow through and consequences
• Integrity

Finally, you should read any agreement you fill out on behalf of your child with him or her before signing. Whether it's an electronics contract for school or a sports team's behavior and grades policy, an online user agreement or form to join a site or get an app(go over together). We teach our kids to be responsible when we teach them to read everything they sign and that their signature is their promise.

Filling out forms teaches responsibility.

29

Paying It Forward: Making the World a Better Place

We want our kids to do good. How do you raise kids who will help a neighbor, think of those less fortunate than them, and do a good deed every once in a while? Teach them while thcy're young. Homework and practice teach children personal responsibility. Chores teach good family citizenship. Good deeds are our chance to make the world a better place. Here is a guide for picking the activities that make sense for your family and forming this habit early.

1. **Giving stuff.**

   - **Understand better the lifecycle of "want."** What do I mean? Well, you can tell your son that the toy or game or device he deeeeeesperately wants will not be so interesting to him in a few months. He won't actually believe you, but you can tell him. Or you can let him learn this lesson by inventorying his stuff with him every once in a while. Sometimes this will reignite an interest, sometimes a child will agree that his interest has waned. Either way, the child starts thinking, "If I'm not using this, maybe someone else can." This also encourages another important skill: "cleaning out."
   - **Learn about "want" versus "need."** It is a good idea to require some sacrifice of our children. They shouldn't only be encouraged to give away stuff that no longer has value to them. I know, I know ... the whining! But giving is important, both for others and for its own sake. What does a kid learn by giving up

something she still occasionally likes, or one of something she is collecting, or anything else she might have? She learns humility ("I am not the center of the universe") and that giving helps and helping matters.

ASK DOCTOR G

Parent Q: For my daughter's sixth birthday I was struck by a wave of momentary insanity and agreed to invite her whole class for a party. Then it hit me: 33 birthday gifts. Now this seems like a terrible idea. What should I do?

*A*sk your daughter to pick six friends who will get her a gift. Ask the rest of the kids to bring a gift to benefit your daughter's choice of charity. Maybe she is very interested in sports. Find a school in your area that would like some new sports equipment but can't afford to make those purchases. Ask that everyone bring a piece of sports equipment that will be donated (and doesn't need to be wrapped). If this is your daughter's school, great. She will get to benefit as well from the donations. If it is not her school, she will learn about the power of bringing a group together and doing good. Then, contact the parents of the six kids she has chosen and explain, asking them to bring a gift for her instead. Some of the parents you contacted might send a gift and a donation. Go with the flow here.

A couple of days after her party, gather up all the donations and your daughter and go to the school that could use the stuff. Contact the gym teacher, principal, or whomever you are delivering to beforehand. Let the contact person know what your daughter did regarding her birthday gifts and that you'd like to bring her along to deliver them. This is a memorable experience. Do something like this again next year. And feel free to praise her for her good deed, even though it wasn't her idea. After all, those were her presents!

2. Giving money.

Giving money is a valuable way to help the world be a better place. For example, around Thanksgiving most schools do a food drive, or a toy drive, or a warm clothes drive. The easiest thing to do is to buy something, put it in your child's backpack, and remind him to hand it in at school. Actually, the easiest thing to do is grab a can of something that has been in your pantry for months or years and put it in the backpack. But here is a great opportunity.

- **Preschoolers.** Engage them in the decision making about what to give. Teach some empathy. Imagine a four-year-old in a family that doesn't have enough money for a great Thanksgiving dinner. What would you want to make sure they have so they really enjoy the day? Stuffing? Pie? A coloring book for the four-year-old while the parents are getting dinner ready? Don't be afraid to let your children know that hard stuff happens to families. They will find it much less of a shock when unpleasant or downright hard things happen to them in life. And they may gain a little extra appreciation for their own good fortune.

- **Elementary schoolers.** Partner with them in purchasing the items. Yes, I mean have them give some money of their own. In our house we have a matching policy. If one of our sons chooses to make a donation, we match it dollar for dollar. When the school said "Dress Down for Breast Cancer" (which is not as racy as it sounds—they have a uniform and just want to wear jeans) if kids bring $1, then our son needs to fish 50 cents out of his piggy bank or come up with a way to earn it. If we hand him the money, our son is merely the delivery person—he's not actually doing a good deed.

- **Middle schoolers.** When your child feels strongly enough to fork over her own money for a good cause, encourage her to try a little fundraising. Reach out to an adult or two with the story of what and why she is giving, and see if your child can motivate someone else to match her efforts as well.

As I mentioned in Chapter 26 on allowance, kids learn a lot by setting aside a portion of "their" money for donations. The other way our kids will learn to budget some money for good works is if they see us doing the same. We just can't get out of a darned thing, can we?

3. Giving time.

Often, kids have more time than money. Even if that's not true, even if time is your child's most precious commodity, teach him to give a little away. Again, there are several lessons to be learned here. Remember when I said that if you have a child who thinks *want* equals *need*, she may learn a lesson by finding something she can give up? The same is true of time. If you have a child who has a packed schedule but finds some time in there to volunteer helping others, he may find that his schedule is more flexible than he thought. Also, the experiences during the act of volunteering can't be replaced.

I have a friend with three adult sons. When they were growing up, they felt lots of pressure to get stuff: sports stuff, tech stuff, they "needed" lots of things. One day my friend stopped lecturing and refusing and made an appointment instead at the Unity Kitchen. She took her boys with her to set the tables and serve the food to over 200 women and their kids as they came in for dinner and then tried to find a bed at this homeless shelter where each spot was first-come first-serve every day. She answered any questions they had but didn't give any speeches. She said the "gimmies" dropped off considerably after that, for some months. They took to doing this several times a year, from the time her youngest was six years old.

Want to avoid having children who grow up to be entitled teens and young adults? Give them opportunities to learn for themselves how lucky they are. It works much better than telling them that.

4. Giving skills.

Here is another opportunity for attracting two birds with one song. Donating a skill teaches compassion and humility while at the same time building self-esteem. What craziness is this? If your son has a great voice, he should spend some time "practicing" his singing by performing at a retirement home in your community. If your daughter builds Legos better than anyone you know, have her drag her huge box of Legos to a nearby after-school program and spend some time teaching what she knows to younger kids.

Every child has something that comes more easily to him. Find that skill and exploit it for good. You're teaching your child to give of himself and also how special he is. Age is no barrier here. Your youngest smiley kiddo can go play in the lobby of that retirement home and make older people smile just by being there. If you point out that this was a good deed, he will see that it is. Does your daughter change clothes 17 times in a morning, each outfit more creative and outrageous than the last? Make up a show, ask a few of her friends to join in, and take it to a children's hospital or adult daycare program.

Do you have a child so shy that any of this would be torture? Then find a way to volunteer in a more solitary way. Perhaps that child loves animals and could volunteer to pet and care for animals. Maybe your shy one is pretty organized and would like to pack bags alone with you at the food pantry. Or the two of you could make decorations at home and donate them to an organization for any holiday that is meaningful to you.

Here's the bottom line: I'm not letting you off the hook. Giving is the right thing to do, and it will help you raise the kind of kids you admire. This will help you avoid raising teenagers who think the whole world is there merely to serve them. Don't look for reasons not to do this. Look for opportunities, large or small, to make giving as normal for your children as playing.

Sometime in the next 10 or 15 years, our parents are likely to spend some time in the hospital, recovering from a fall or an illness. When they need this level of care that we, as their children, can't give them, there will be people there to help them. Those med techs and nurses' aides will bathe and help them dress, answer their calls for assistance, and see to their comforts. Most of the people who will do this for our parents in the future are children now. Let's teach those children compassion and charity. Let's raise a generation that can look beyond themselves.

30

Take Your (Actual) Medicine

Have you heard of pharm parties? This is when (back in the day) teens would bring a handful (each) of whatever prescription meds they could find and dump them into one big bowl. They all mix together and then each person takes a handful and downs them, usually with an alcoholic chaser. This is only one example of the strange and terrifying behaviors surrounding medication abuse.

We all want our someday-teenagers to be responsible about health, medication, and drug use. How do we get there? In the years leading up to that time, our kids need to learn:

- How to manage allergies they have.

- Who needs to know about their medical problems (if any).

- Which medicine they are supposed to take.

- When (and how) to take medicine.

- Where to keep their medicine so other kids can't try it.

- What medicine is for, and what it's not.

- Why to avoid medicine unless it's prescribed by a doctor and agreed to by a parent.

How do they learn all this? In steps.

Toddlers.

➤ Allergies? Teach the name. A food allergy is life-saving information. When an adult asks, "Is anyone allergic to anything?" your child should practice raising a hand and saying "Peanuts!" even if you've already informed everyone in a six-mile radius about her allergy.

➤ Daily medicine? Build this into the daily routine at a predictable time so your little one will know how important it is to remember.

Preschoolers.

➤ Allergies? Time for kids to learn to advocate for themselves. Start the very slow transition from controlling everything your child touches to giving her some responsibility for keeping herself safe. Four-year-olds can learn:

- To ask before eating.

- Where the EpiPen is kept.

➤ Medical issues? Under supervision, your preschooler can:

- Learn the name of his medicine and reason for needing it.

- Get his own medicine and take it.

Ages 5–7.

➤ Learn medicine rules:

- Keep medicines up high.

- Only take it if an adult agrees that you need it.

- Never share it.

➤ Teach kids to share their own medical issues responsibly. Who needs to know about a medical problem? A coach, a teacher, maybe a friend's parent. Involve your children in your decision making and informing.

Ages 8–10.

➤ It's time to talk about how medicines can cause problems. Too much, too little, wrong time, wrong person, a healthy respect for medicines as a tool can save kids' lives.

➤ Build empathy and help kids learn to balance safety and privacy. When is the right time to ask a question about someone else's health? How can we reach out to help someone in ways that are respectful?

Ages 11–12.

➤ Drugs versus medicine. Middle schoolers are usually aware that some people use substances without adult permission. Sharing ADHD or other medications is too common even in kids this young. Talk often with your kids about why people might do this and why it's a terrible idea.

➤ Children with chronic medical issues or allergies often reject those constraints at this age. Their desire to be more like their peers can cause some very dangerous behaviors as they stop taking medicine, push against restrictions, and lie to themselves and others about their health. Showing empathy for their frustration but holding them accountable for mature behavior is the only way I've seen through this minefield with the fewest complications.

Most everyone needs to take medicine at some time or another. Teaching our children while they are young will help them use medicine sparingly and appropriately.

31

How Can I Help? What Else Can I Do?

There's a "Free to Be ... You and Me" song that describes two kinds of help: the kind that *actually* helps and the kind "we all can do without!" You're having a birthday party for one of your kids at home. A friend comes over to help set up. You first ask the friend to clear off the coffee table. You are cooking, arranging, answering the phone, and after a while you realize your friend never came back. The coffee table is sort of cleared off, and she is sitting in the living room updating her Facebook status. That kind of help can make you nuts.

Most of us teach our kids to help. Starting with "clean up, clean up, everybody clean up" in preschool, our children learn to pitch in. We can't anticipate every opportunity our children will have or be there with them always to encourage them to help in a useful way. So teach them these two phrases and they will be good to go.

"How can I help?"

Every time your kids see you doing something that is for the greater good, like carrying groceries, folding laundry, or fixing something, encourage them to ask this question. At least half the time the answer will be "Nothing, thanks!" But it feels good to be asked, and it's responsible to offer. Then encourage them to do the same thing at school or at a friend's house. This is a great way to make sure other adults like your children, which is never a bad thing. It makes them better guests, students, employees, friends, and even someday a better spouse.

"What else can I do?"

This is really the key. Teach your child that every time she starts to help someone, she ends the task by going back to the person in charge and saying, "What else can I do?" If you've ever worked at a job or on a project with a group of people, you know that this is the best sign that someone is a good worker. This person will be the last to be laid off in tough economic times because the boss can count on her. This person will also advance the fastest toward their goals.

We teach the "What else can I do?" lesson at our house this way: When someone comes home with groceries, we call all the boys out to the car. They start trooping in with the bags. They keep coming back out until it's all inside, and then ask, "What else can I do?" Usually I say, "Nothing, thanks! You're excused." But if one of them fades away after bringing in a bag or two without checking in, all the rest of his brothers are excused because that boy will be carrying in *and* putting away all the groceries. Believe me when I tell you that this lesson sticks after the first time!

As adults, we know that this attitude is job security in a sentence. The tough part is the consistency we need to teach this lesson in every "helping" situation. I promise it's worth it. As you plan out your day, or find yourself with a list of chores, look for opportunities to build your child's work ethic in this way. You'll be really glad you did.

PART III

RESILIENCE
RAISING PROBLEM SOLVERS

32

Resilience: Take One Step Back

Come back in time with me. It's the first day of the school year a few years ago, and our first- and third-graders are thrilled to take the bus home from school for the very first time. They've both memorized the name of the bus (purple). They know to wait for us at the bus stop.

As 3:30 nears, my husband and I stick the two-year-old in the stroller and walk down with him and the four-year-old to meet the bus. The corner is lovely, the traffic pretty quiet. We wait. And wait. Not that worried, really; first-day buses usually leave late and arrive late as the driver and the teachers sort out who goes where. Just as we're starting to seriously wonder, my cell phone rings. It's the eight-year-old, calling from our two-doors-down neighbor's house. "Can you come home and let us in, please?"

What?! Well, the bus dropped off the children on the right street, but on a completely different corner, over a hill from where we were waiting. The boys waited and waited, but we didn't come. So they held hands, carefully crossed the street, then walked up the hill and around a different corner, right to our house … where we weren't. Our next-door neighbors weren't home either, our son explained, but the neighbors next to them were home and let the boys use the phone.

That mix-up made a huge impression on our kids. Whenever anything didn't go according to plan for the rest of the school year, they'd say, "We can handle it." And that included the time that the six-year-old fell asleep on the bus and didn't get off when his older brother did.

That mix-up also taught me a big lesson. As a parent, I often want everything to go perfectly, especially the first time my kids tackle something new. When things do go perfectly, I feel a huge sense of relief, and often a sense of accomplishment as well. But what do my kids learn? They learn they can handle life if everything goes as planned.

Resilience means learning how to handle life when nothing goes as planned.

Every challenge our kids face is a chance to learn resilience. Here is the path:

1. **A child has an expectation about an experience.** This might be an event or a relationship or an activity, or just any particular day. The child has a picture (vague or specific) about how it will go.

2. **Something unexpected happens.** Suddenly that child goes from cruising along to actively feeling and thinking. Occasionally, the unexpected is wonderful (a snow day, or a surprise visit from a friend), but usually it's stressful in some way. Humans—little or big—don't often like having their expectations thwarted.

3. **Strong emotion comes out.** When we feel angry, scared, hurt, or other strong and negative emotions, that overwhelms the reasoning part of our brain for a little while. That amount of time might be a few seconds or many minutes. The first task a child must learn is to move through the emotion to a calmer place. This is, in particular, the hard work toddlers spend so much time doing.

4. **There are choices to be made.** Young children decide what adult to enlist for help. Older kids have to think about how they want to proceed. They have to identify the options and pick one.

5. **Each choice has consequences.** Kids are constantly learning from their choices.

This pattern plays out over and over again. Our hardest job as parents is to get out of the way when our kids face challenges. Our main role is to watch, listen, and offer some guidance. When we interfere as little as possible in this cycle, our kids will gain confidence. Out of confidence grows true self-esteem. Instead of telling our children

"Good job!" they can experience for themselves how it feels to do a good job, and how to be resilient.

We all know we learn from experience, and we all want our kids to be able to handle whatever life throws at them. So why don't we get out of the way?

Love, fear, and guilt.

We **love** these little beings so much. We want them to be happy, to have the best, easiest, most wonderful lives possible. We want to give them the benefit of our greater resources and greater experience. We have such empathy for their harder emotions, and gain such pleasure when life is going their way.

Our **fears** are wrapped tightly around our children and what might happen to them. We feel (and should) such responsibility for our children, to protect them and shield them. It's so easy to feel overwhelmed when life challenges a child, and to see how quickly a situation might deteriorate if it's not solved immediately. As adults, the future consequences of trouble can seem huge. And, even when we're strong enough to picture stepping back and letting our child fail in order to learn, we fear risking our child's love.

Finally, and most powerfully, I think we are quick to experience guilt. Parents feel guilt for working too much or not working enough, outside the home; for having only one child or for having too many kids; for making a choice a child doesn't like or for giving the child everything she requests. Parents are capable of feeling guilty for pretty much everything. So, the guilt we feel if we even consider not rescuing a child when we could? Monstrous!

Given all that pressure, how can we possibly let them fall?

When should we step in to help?

Sometimes jumping in is more than compassion, it's life-saving. Sometimes the fear we feel is spot-on, and we must stand between our children and true physical or emotional danger. Here are a few questions to ask yourself in that moment:

✓ Is a life in danger? We should not build resilience by letting a child cross the street alone who doesn't yet have the skills. I mean this literally.

✓ Is the scary outcome you fear actually likely? My best friend uses what she calls "the 11 o'clock News test." If I heard of another parent who let his or her child do this thing and it made it on the news, would I think "What a terrible parent!" or would I think, "That could've happened to anyone"?

✓ If this ends badly, is there something valuable to be learned?

If your child is being bullied or victimized in some way, step in and defend your child. If there is a serious health risk to your child, you have to take an active role. But what if none of those things are true?

Whenever you can, take one step back.

I'm not asking you to step out of the picture. I'm asking you to protect your child from behind. What in the world does *that* mean? Use this resilience-building challenge as a way to strengthen your child for the next challenge, and the next. Let her see that you have faith in her ability to problem solve.

1. **Be interested.** Something didn't go according to your child's expectations. You're not stepping back because you don't care; you're stepping back because you do!

2. **Listen with empathy.** Those strong emotions are important to your child, so they are important to you.

3. **Express faith in your child's ability** to approach this struggle with good ideas. Ask what options he is considering.

4. **Don't tell him what to do!** This. Is. The. Hardest. Part. You can offer an opinion if he presses you for one, but don't volunteer. This is the difference between doing a project yourself and turning in someone else's work. No matter what the grade, you know you didn't do it.

5. **Be interested in what happens.** If we don't give advice then we don't have to fight back an I-told-you-so. We can concentrate on, "What did you learn?"

There are a lot of ways to teach kids resilience. This section lists a bunch, and my activity books have dozens more. But the best way for children to learn that they can handle trouble is to practice. So we have to give them the opportunity, over and over again.

33

Find Resilience Opportunities

Resilience is the ability to overcome adversity. If it were actually possible to protect our kids from every bad thing that might ever happen to them for their entire lives, then I would be writing about how to do that. Since it absolutely is not possible, I believe that parents (as well as grandparents, educators, caregivers, and all loving adults) have the obligation to teach kids how to handle life when it doesn't go their way. Because it often won't.

Watch kids running and jumping on a playground. One falls down and looks for her parent. If the parent says, "Hey, you're OK!" the child believes. Up she gets, toddles over for a boo-boo kiss, and then off she goes to play again. When something happens to a toddler that is new or scary or uncertain, he looks to his grown-up to understand how to feel.

Older children do the same by bringing stories of hurts and difficulties to a parent for the postgame dissection: "He did this, and then I said that, and now I hate him!" Whether it's a friend or teacher or sibling or teammate conflict, kids bring their parents the struggles that come up in life. What can we do in those daily moments that elevate our children?

See it as an opportunity.

Look at each struggle as a chance to raise the child in front of you into the adult you know he can be. Imagine for a moment that you go to your son's kindergarten parent-teacher conference. His teacher tells you that he is doing great, but he is struggling a little with numbers. He often knows the number he is looking at, but he is uncertain of himself and won't answer. She asks you to look for chances in your time together with him to find numbers he can read. Well, sure! You could ask him about the numbers on street signs, menus, and commercials, or maybe get flashcards. And with the extra experience, his confidence would soar.

I am asking you to look for chances in your time together with your kids to find problems they can solve. To look for opportunities to overcome difficulty as you stand one step behind her, not in front of her. I'm asking you to (as has wisely been said many times) prepare your child for the road, rather than trying to prepare the road for your child. The ability to solve life's problems is far more important than the ability to solve math problems.

Our kids will look to us to know if they're OK. And they almost always are. So give them the confidence to try, to fail, to solve. Keep one eye on the child in front of you, and one eye on the adult you are working to raise. Our work as parents is to see the possible paths from one to the other. We can't stand too close if we're going to see that path; we have to step back as often as possible so we can see the big picture.

We have to encourage our kids to be risk-takers, even if this goes against everything we feel when we look at our precious kids. We want to preach caution and care, but that won't teach the resilience they need, or help them achieve their most treasured dreams.

As I struggle with seeing these paths for my own children, a friend (who's a grandma—they give such good advice, don't they?) gave me some wise counsel. I told her, "I can't see the big picture, I am too overwhelmed by the pain my child is feeling." She said, "You're together in a sailboat. You don't have to be able to see the shore, but you do have to keep the boat pointed in the correct direction. That means having enough perspective to know where you're trying to go."

Think of two people you know who have both lived through (or live with) tough circumstances. Over a decade ago, I took care of two different female patients, both in their 50s. One had a progressive disease that left her wheelchair-bound and unable to move anything but her head. The other had some mild back pain.

One day I walked into an exam room to see the first woman. "How are you?" I asked. "Wonderful! My grandson turned one this weekend and we had such a nice party, and the roses are coming up in my garden. I'm going to a concert later this week, and I'm really looking forward to it!"

Later that day I saw the second woman. "How are you?" I asked. "Just terrible, as usual. I never know if my back will hurt, so it might as well hurt all the time because I can't make any plans or get anything done."

Resilience is the secret sauce. Standing up to adversity requires tools, resources, and experience, of course. It also requires a resilient attitude.

- Knowing that one has the tools, or can find them.

- The ability to look for resources and gather them to aid you.

- The experience to know that you can manage in the face of difficulty, that feelings can change with time, and that life is what you make it.

A few lucky kids are born resilient. Nothing seems to bother them or keep them down. The rest of us need to work on it. When you look at a child who is easily hurt or tender of heart, you might think, "I need to protect him from difficulty." I challenge that assumption! If you had a child who struggled with reading, would you think, "I need to protect her from having to read" or would you search for ways to teach her?

So we should toss our kids to the wolves just to see how they handle it? Nope, I'm not saying that either.

What does work?

- Kids learn resilience when they solve problems. We don't need to give our kids problems to solve; we just need to stop jumping in to solve their problems for them.

- Confidence is crucial. When we step back and let kids try, we show our faith in them. Our belief that they can find an answer, and that they can handle themselves if things go wrong.

- Understand that resilience is not an emotion. We don't need
  to tell our kids how to feel (and it doesn't work when we try).
  Resilience is about action, and can exist no matter what kids feel.

Once, after I spoke to a large group about resilience, a woman approached me with a story: "My dad passed away about five years ago, and you've really improved my memories of him." How? This woman was raised on a farm with four siblings. Mom was a teacher in town, but Dad was always around, working on the farm. Whenever one of the teens in the family had a problem, he or she would go out and sit on the tractor and talk to him about it. No matter what the problem, he'd listen patiently and then say, "Well, that's a pretty fine fix you've gotten yourself into there, kiddo. I'll be interested to see how you get yourself out."

She went on to explain that this phrase had become a joke in their family; to this day, if one of the grandkids spilled something or came in with a complaint at a family party, the siblings would give that same answer, in unison, and laugh. "But now you've got me thinking," she said to me. "Maybe our dad had it right. After all, we're all employed, thriving adults who can handle our own problems."

Isn't that our main parenting goal?

34

Get Off the Happiness Hook

Brace yourself. This is the most liberating concept in this whole book. It will change your life, and help you see that you are a much better parent than you feel like most days. Also, it will enable you to make your children even greater people, with a much better shot at a fulfilling life.

Stop trying to make your kids happy.

We have to let ourselves off the happiness hook. Ignore the online headlines, the magazine articles, even our friends' questions. We have to understand what happiness is, and what it is not.

Your child's happiness is *his* responsibility. It is not:

• Guaranteed
• Your priority
• The measure of your parenting success

You've never met my five year old, but you could guess how to make him happy, right? Cartoon Network and a Snicker's bar would make him happy as can be. But those of us who have to live with him, not-so-much. And if we give that to him every day, to make sure he's always happy? Think of the kind of kid he would become. If we did that, I'm pretty sure you wouldn't want him to be friends with your child, or date your teenager, or be your employee, or push your mom in a wheelchair someday in the hospital.

Happiness is not the point of childhood. It is often a lucky by-product, but it is not the purpose and should not be our main parenting goal.

You might be thinking, "This woman doesn't want her kids to be happy? Ack!" That is not the case at all. I like my kids most days, very much. I hope they will be happy often. Partially this is selfish. My kids are a lot more fun to be around when they're happy. But I want that happiness to be created by them. My point here is not to deny them happiness, it's to stop worrying about it.

Why shouldn't we try to make our kids happy?

1. Because we can't. You can't actually make someone else happy in the long run. You can smooth the way, solve all the problems, protect them from as many harsh moments or difficulties as you can see, but they will still feel some pain.

2. Unhappiness teaches. Did you ever say something mean about a friend? If the friend finds out, she confronts you or ditches you. Next time you are more likely to speak kindly, and part of that is remembering how unhappy you were when you got called out on your bad behavior. Doesn't your child need to learn similar lessons?

3. Happiness is hard. If you judge your parenting by your child's happiness, you'll feel like a failure some days. If you judge your parenting by your child's growth and learning, you can succeed any day you choose.

I know this sounds crazy. Our goal as parents is not to furnish a fleeting sense of satisfaction to our children. Instead, our goal as parents is to raise our kids to find and create their own happiness. What if, instead of asking ourselves, "Is my child happy?" we start asking, "Is my child learning and growing?"

35

Asking for Help

You know what most parents are terrible at doing? Asking for help. We might wish for help, imagine what it would be like if we just had a little help, even be angry about not getting enough help. But asking? Nope. We just don't do it often, or well.

Resilience means asking for help. A problem solver reaches out to find resources, and most often those resources are people.

When you take your kids on an outing, start first by having them identify the "experts" in that setting. Who works there? How can they tell? If your family has a question, how will you get it answered? Who can help? Most importantly, talk about what your child should do if he gets separated from you.

When my sons were five and seven, we were at a baseball stadium. They went in to use the bathroom together (same stall—I'm *that* mom in a public place), and when they finished they came back out ... the other door, the door that none of us knew was there. Naturally, we got separated. When the little one asked the bigger one, "Wow, you know how to get back to our seats?" the older one replied, "Actually? No. But I bet that security guard can help us." The security guard did help, taking them to guest relations where the boys could report my name (make sure your child knows yours) and cell phone number. We were reunited very quickly. It may have felt like three years to me, but ended up only taking about five minutes.

Toddlers.

➢ Teach the connection between feeling frustrated and getting assistance.

➢ Ask your child for help with simple tasks: "Will you help me with this towel? It goes in the laundry basket."

Preschoolers.

➢ Talk about the difference between "help" and "do it for me!" Help is a child doing her best and getting aid for only the parts she can't yet do herself.

➢ In a positive way, point out when you're helping your child. "I'm happy to help you do this. I like how you are trying your best."

Ages 5–7.

➢ Ask about getting help at school—when should someone go to the teacher?

➢ Praise examples of problem solving through asking for assistance.

Ages 8–10.

➢ Watch some TV together. Notice when a character has a problem that could have been solved by asking the right person for help.

➢ Homework struggle? Encourage your child to find another way (besides asking you) to get the help he needs. Homework help lines, e-mailing a teacher, or calling a classmate are all valuable resources that provide great practice.

Ages 11–12.

➤ Encourage your child to be a tutor, assistant coach, or mentor for a younger or less experienced person. Understanding how great it feels to help someone else can make it easier when we need to turn to someone for assistance ourselves.

➤ Talk about your own requests for help. Tweens really listen. Show yours that you mean it when you say asking for help is resilient, and admirable, by giving examples of getting support when you need it. Which means, of course, that we have to actually do that.

36

"I'm Booooooooorrrrrreeeed!": Free Time Management

I love boredom.

Not for me, since I'm never bored (thank you smartphone). But I love it for my kids. Why? Boredom teaches:

• Curiosity

• Initiative

• Creativity

• Problem solving

• Resilience

When kids are bored, they have to think: What else would be fun to do? Who is here? How do I get them to play with me? What is around me? What do I like? What won't get me in trouble? What would get me in trouble? Is it worth it?

It is so frustrating for parents when our kids come to us complaining there's "nothing to do." Am I raising spoiled brats? Don't they see this home full of toys? How can they be bored? I'd LOVE to have nothing to do for an hour!

We're used to fixing problems for our kids, and the solutions are so obvious to us. We suggest games, offer toys, mention activities. We drop what we're doing to arrange playdates, go on outings, and rearrange the day to stop the horror of boredom.

Here is a radical suggestion: Don't solve this problem for your kids. For younger kids, we can guide them a little. For older kids? Well, read on:

Toddlers.

➤ First, we have to teach them to recognize what they're feeling. Toddlers usually "solve" boredom by getting into things they know they're not supposed to touch. Explain, "You're done with what you were doing? OK, put it away and show me what toy you'll play with next." In line or waiting for something? Ask them to look around, and find things such as colors, numbers, and shapes. Waiting rooms and restaurants are filled with interesting items to notice.

Preschoolers.

➤ Create an activities basket. This is especially handy for times when you are busy with a younger sibling, working on a child's bath or nap, or feeding the baby. A box of items the older child can get out and work on alone will increase his feeling of independence and autonomy while fueling creativity.

Ages 5–7.

➤ Keep an activity list. When your child has lots of ideas for things to do, or doesn't get to something she wanted to do, ask her to put it on a list. Encourage her to go back to that list when she's searching for something fun to do. This builds resilience as she learns to create a resource for herself to solve a future problem.

Ages 8–10.

➤ Older elementary children are absolutely able to (after you give permission) start making their own plans for playdates with friends. Teach the skills of problem solving and planning ahead by encouraging your son to call friends and schedule time together. He'll need to look at (and understand) his schedule, present a plan to you, get approval, and get on the phone.

➤ This is the right age to start phasing out of helping to solve this problem. If kids this age come to you for ideas, give them something from your own chores list. "Clean the bathroom" is my favorite.

Ages 11–12.

By this age, I have all kinds of creative answers to "There is nothing to do!" These include, but are not limited to:

➤ Go through all your clothes and put the ones that don't fit in a box.

➤ Get ahead on next week's homework.

➤ Wash the kitchen floor.

➤ Take your little brother to the playground.

➤ The basement needs to be cleaned out.

Clearly, these are designed to make *my* life easier. See why I love boredom? And do you get why my children slap their hands over the mouths of friends who even start to complain about not having anything to do at our house?

We need our kids to experience boredom a little more often. To accomplish that, we have to turn off the screens sometimes. Turning one on is a great boredom-buster, but we want our kids to learn to think further than that.

As we strive to raise resilient humans, this is an easy place to stop jumping in to help our children. They can solve this problem, and we can mention at dinner how interested we are to see how they managed.

37

Playdates and Sleepovers and Trips, Oh My!

The simple truth is that our kids need to learn to be away from us. It's been said before that parenting is a job where we work to put ourselves out of a job. In the midst of teaching our kids to listen to us and respect us, we have to teach them—slowly—to stop needing us in their daily lives. This process takes many years.

The best way to tackle this goal is with the help of other adults you know and trust. Kids need community so that they can try out tiny bits of independence and adventure. Those tiny bits lead to confidence and problem solving, after which they are ready for a little more.

Toddlers.

Our youngest kids often have trouble letting a caregiver go to the bathroom. That instinct, to keep a trusted grown-up in sight at all times, is protective. So we start very slowly.

➢ **It's OK to pee alone.** A child needs to be in a safe place, and some toddlers are remarkably quick at finding any chink in the armor of your child-proofing. My heights-loving child had to be stuck in his playpen for the 60 seconds a trip to the bathroom took me. And yes, he did yell, but he survived, and so did I.

➢ **If you trust someone, take a break.** The first step in learning to venture away from you is having a babysitter: a relative, a friend, or a paid sitter. Your child may put up a huge fuss, and that is normal. Go out anyway. She will slowly learn that she is OK for a little while without you there.

Preschoolers.

Four- and five-year-olds are ready for a little bit more adventure. They still need child-proofing, but are less likely to chew on the electrical cords. These children usually

➢ **Can play in a room by themselves.** Some kids are born with this skill, but many need to practice it and start with very short experiences. In a safe space, challenge your little one to put together an activity list or box and play while you do something in another room. Praise his resilience, especially if he handles a problem on his own.

➢ **Need friends.** As I mentioned before, friends teach resilience. In addition to that, friends are a great pull away from family, and will encourage kids to get a little bit outside their comfort zones. Try a new game, such as an adventure around the backyard or park. Have your child stay within her comfortable boundaries, but remember to stretch those boundaries a little to build that skill of being on her own.

Ages 5–7.

Just as kids this age are learning to listen to the teacher and be at school without you, they are ready for a little bit more social adventuring as well.

➢ **Playdates build resilience.** Going to a friend's house means learning a new set of rules and reacting to a new group of people. When minor injuries or disappointments happen, your child will find that he can (often) get through the hard time on his own.

Knowing that he can survive a setback and find a solution teaches him that he is strong.

➤ **Teach her to cross the street.** It's almost certainly not yet time for your child to cross the street alone. However, she needs to know what you know about traffic and street-crossing. Explain to her your decision-making process, and start to ask her opinion about when it's safe to cross a street. By age seven, your child should be able to guide you safely at an intersection. Make sure she takes you by the hand!

Ages 8–10.

Get to know the families of your child's friends as well as you can. They will be the source of a lot of your kiddo's resilience-learning opportunities.

➤ **Outings with other adults.** Does Grandma want to take your children to see a matinee? Is the coach springing for pizza after the game? Is there a youth group field trip to a farm? If this adult is trusted, let your children go. Ask them what they learned, and what problems they found. Then find out from your problem solver what happened next.

➤ **Sleepovers.** Many parents have a strict policy against sleepovers, but I'm a huge fan. Hosting them is a great way to get to know your child's friends, and for him to build stronger relationships. Letting your child sleep somewhere else makes some parents VERY nervous. If you have been through a bad experience, then you must heed your gut. There is a chance that something scary could happen to or around your child. But that possibility is slim if you ask some good questions first. The probability is great that your child will have a great learning and growing experience. Definitely have guidelines to decide what situations are acceptable.

  • **Know the other family!** Be comfortable asking all the following questions, as well as whatever other questions are on your mind. If you can't ask, or do not trust that you'll get an honest answer, your child is not sleeping over at that house.

- **Ask "Who will be around?"** This is good because you never know who is visiting, if there will be a sitter, or even if an older child is having friends over who might bring a different element to the experience.

- **Ask "What are the plans?"** You may want to ask about the rating of the movie they'll watch, or how late they'll be out with the kids, or any number of things.

- **Ask "Do you have any rules you want me to let my child know about?"** That way, if you hear, "Yes, please tell him the boys are not allowed to play with our gun collection in the pool after the sitter goes home if we're not back from the bar," you can perhaps reevaluate your decision about the sleepover.

ASK DOCTOR G

Parent Q: I don't know if my child is ready for a sleepover. What if he goes and then calls at bedtime crying to come home?

*F*irst sleepovers can take a few tries, and many kids think they are ready to be away from you all night before they actually are. Before he goes, do your best to set him up for success. Pick a home he is completely comfortable in, somewhere he has spent lots of time without you. Talk to the adult (his grandparent or best friend's parent) about this first experience and, away from his ears, prepare them for the chance he'll want to go home. Then make sure he knows your number.

If he calls and you can't easily soothe him over the phone? Go pick him up. Not only is that the loving thing to do, you are teaching him a great lesson for later. Someday he may be in a circumstance where he is being bullied or being asked to do something against his better judgment. Knowing that a call home is a reliable escape route could save him from a very bad situation.

Ages 11–12.

Often tweens are ready for *any* outing that does not include their own parents. If that is true for your child, take advantage of the learning opportunity.

➤ **Trips.** If your child is lucky enough to get invited to be away overnight for a school function or with a friend's family, seriously consider letting her go. Ask the questions you need to ask to be confident that there is a small chance of big risk, and then look at the big chance of great learning. Encourage your child's adventurous spirit.

➤ **Sleepaway camp.** This is not possible for every family, and for many parents it's a crazy idea. For a lot of tweens it's a crazy idea as well. But if your child is interested, and your family has the opportunity—whether it's a sports camp or Girl Scouts or VBS or any other sleepaway experience—there is no end to the learning and growing that tweens and teens can do at camp.

Take a moment to think back on your own childhood. Do you remember solving a big problem or getting through a new experience without your parent there to help? Often these are the most profound life lessons we encountered.

As we slowly teach our kids to leave us, they need to try it. It's not enough to tell them we know they can do it. We have to give them the understanding to see that they have left us a bit at a time, and thrived doing it.

38

Mom, She's Bugging Me!: Sibling Management

Is there any better relationship for building resilience than brothers and sisters? Complete familiarity, 24/7 access, and painful honesty lead to some of the most unflinching feedback our kids will ever get about who they are, how they look, and what they do. If that doesn't teach you to stand up in the face of adversity, what will?

ASK·DOCTOR G

Parent Q: My kids argue, but I'm starting to wonder if my eight-year-old is actually bullying my 11-year-old. Can siblings (especially a younger) bully? Or is it just normal fighting?

Sibling bullying absolutely happens. Further, it is entirely normal. However, that does not make it *at all* acceptable. Bullying is what happens when a child experiments with social power. Using words, threats, or physical pain, one child tries to manipulate another to do what he or she wants. Almost every child tries this, and often on a sibling. As you watch your children interact with each other at home, you're right to be vigilant against bullying. Most children try this social power

(continued)

ASK DOCTOR G

(*continued*)

first on siblings. Here's a test to decide if what you're seeing is bullying or bickering:

1. Imagine the interaction you are witnessing at home taking place in public.
2. Replace your own child who is being controlling with a child you don't know.
3. Would you call it bullying?

If the answer is yes, then the answer is yes even when it is one of your own kids with another of your own kids. Bullying is not OK! especially at home.

Usual sibling arguing and bickering.

Have you checked to make sure this is not bullying? If so, do your best to remove yourself from the fray. There are specific things we can do to encourage great relationships, but there is no benefit to micromanaging our kids' relationships with each other. Think of your own siblings. Patterns get established at a pretty young age. If the pattern is to escalate until a parent jumps in, they will struggle to have a strong relationship when they are adults.

Focusing on positive interactions and keeping your kids accountable for their own relationships in the home will give them the resilience they need to stay connected throughout their lives.

Toddlers.

Two- and three-year-olds are incredibly self-serving little beings with moments of staggering empathy and kindness. Appreciate the kindness (out loud) and encourage siblings to do the same. Don't protect little ones from the emotional consequences of their actions toward siblings. If a toddler treats a sibling badly, and the older child is not willing to play for a while, that teaches a stronger lesson than any time-out chair.

> **Jealousy.** Toddlers believe that equal is the same thing as fair, but we know better. If you are taking time "away" from a toddler for a baby's needs, be sure to point out when you are focusing on the toddler. I have been known to say to a (sleeping) baby: "You'll have to wait, I'm reading to your brother right now." If a toddler feels jealous of an older sibling, encourage your little one to express that feeling and suggest an activity for the two of you to plan together.

> **Hitting.** Not OK, ever. Kids this age can't even wrestle with other siblings for more than a minute without it getting out of hand, and they will have no idea how that happened. The rules about keeping hands to oneself need to be clear at this age.

> **Trouble with sharing.** Sharing is hard. Sharing toys, books, space, and parents is a struggle. Teach clear rules. For example, if one child has a toy and the other child wants it, have the second child request a turn. The answer has to be either "Yes" or "In two minutes." Set a timer (or teach the child to do so) and the toy gets turned over at the end of two minutes. If the toy gets snatched before then, the child's turn is forfeited. If the toy isn't turned over at the two-minute mark, a parent helps and then that child gets extra time. Be consistent and children will learn to enforce these rules without your help.

Preschoolers.

Children at these ages can start to understand the intricacies of the sibling dynamic. This means that they will begin to experiment with manipulating siblings and parents to get what they want from a brother or sister. This happens toward older siblings and twins, not only toward younger siblings. Keep the idea that everyone deserves to be treated with respect by everyone in your home.

> **Telling versus tattling.** Be clear with your children that "telling" is letting an adult know if someone is being physically or emotionally hurt, or is in real danger. Everything else is tattling. At our house, if someone tattles, that person has to be willing to

take the punishment alongside the person who was ratted out. That is usually enough to convince the kids to work it out without intervention.

➤ **Appreciate kindness.** When your child does something thoughtful for a younger sibling—not just avoiding nastiness, but actually going above and beyond—notice it. Discuss with your preschooler why you're glad the baby has him as a big brother, and determine what kind of sibling he'd like to be.

➤ **Fair versus equal.** This age of concrete reasoning leads to a lot of concrete "record keeping." Our kids can be more worried about fairness than any referee or standardized test moderator. Would it be fair for you to send your four-year-old on an overnight Boy Scout trip just because his 13-year-old brother is going? Of course not, but it would be equal. Don't get sucked into this argument. It will take years for your child to understand that fair and equal are not the same thing in a family.

Ages 5–7.

Siblings are often the favored playmate of a child at this age. At a time when every moment is an opportunity for a game or fun activity, these interactions can be really joyful. These interactions are also chances to test drive behavior elementary school kids are seeing on the playground or with friends.

➤ **Threatening.** This is where bullying begins. "If you don't let me win I'll never play with you again." "You have to give that to me or I'll tell your friends you still cuddle with Mom." This is different than negotiating: "If you don't play tea party with me now, I won't play Legos with you later." The difference is in the intent to hurt, not just to come to a plan that is acceptable to both people. A child who is threatened should bring that to a parent. And the child who is threatening needs some quality time alone.

➤ **Wrestling.** My kids tussle like a pack of tiger cubs. This, though I don't really get it, seems to strengthen their relationships. So lay down a few ground rules.

1. Everyone has to agree before it starts. No surprise attacks.

2. If you've agreed to the activity, you can't then try to get someone else in trouble if you get hurt. Sometimes wrestling leads to injury.

3. Anyone can "tap out" at any time and all play stops. This means hitting the ground or tapping the shoulder of your opponent twice. If someone taps out and the other person doesn't honor it, that means big trouble.

➤ **Copying.** Is there anything more infuriating than having someone repeat everything you say? Is there anything more infuriating than having someone repeat everything you say? Sorry, I couldn't resist. It's OK to have a rule against this. Copying is disrespectful. End of story.

Ages 8–10.

Older elementary schoolers are keen observers. As with every child of every age, they want to be older, so they will mimic what they see older kids doing. They also *may* be ready to start being responsible for a younger sibling when walking to school or an activity, as long as you place clear expectations (and consequences) upon them for behaving in a responsible manner. Check in with both kids regularly.

➤ **Bickering.** If you're sure it's not bullying, the first thing to do is find out if it bothers either of the kids involved or only bothers you. If it bothers one (or both) of them, help them see that this activity takes two, and that it's impressive and effective to just walk away. If they don't mind it, don't recognize it, or are unwilling to stop, try these guidelines:

1. No bickering around other family members. Take it somewhere private.

2. No tattling about bickering. If it gets out of hand, demand a change or step away.

3. If you have tried to handle it these ways and need help, ask an adult.

➤ **Competition.** I have, I swear, heard this sentence in my house: "Yeah? Well I can ... pee straighter than you!" Some kids will compete over anything and everything, even though there are times it is not appropriate to compete. For example, "Who can eat faster" puts your family on the fast track to meet your local paramedics. And "Who can pee first" just isn't pretty for anyone. So there will be times when you will squash the competition by saying, "No, that race is not happening." But overall, this is not something we need to control. Competition teaches resilience. A younger child may hate that she "always" loses. A lot of sibling competition is unfair. However, she does not have to agree to compete. If she agrees, she should work on not being a sore loser. In addition, she should look for opportunities to excel. Being older isn't always an advantage.

➤ **Insulting.** I like to blame television for this. I wonder what parents blamed before television? Children often show remarkable creativity when insulting each other, and are not always wrong. But your children are never right to insult. This one deserves a rule, too. We don't insult each other. Home is a safe place.

Ages 11–12.

Many tweens wish they were only children. As everything starts to annoy them (blame hormones), siblings are the first and pointiest thorns in their sides. Don't let that deter you. Siblings can also be the only people who can reach through a tween's really bad mood and draw out a laugh, a sigh, or the truth about what's bothering him.

➤ **Criticizing.** This can look a lot like insulting, but kids would argue that point. Siblings are really excellent at giving constant, honest feedback. "Are you wearing *that?*" "You sound like a donkey when you laugh and you spit, too!" "Why do you invite that kid over when you ignore her at school?" "I'm not playing that with you, you cheat!" A great deal of this feedback is hard to hear (especially for parents), but very useful for kids. So make your expectations clear:

1. No bullying. Does it start with "No offense, but ..." or some other obvious excuse for disrespect? Is the comment scornful or repeated too often?

2. Give feedback, not criticism. The difference is clear: We give feedback to help someone improve something because we care about her success. We give criticism because we want the satisfaction of proving how much more we know.

3. Offer criticism along with a genuine compliment. If you're too annoyed to do that, it's probably not going to come out right, so keep your mouth shut until you calm down.

➤ **Interfering in friendships.** As tweens struggle with friendships of their own, they often become critical or jealous of siblings' relationships with other kids. Friendships are a lot like possessions—a child can't just snatch the one she wants. She needs to ask for her sibling to share.

➤ **Isolating.** Tweens are pack animals, and they are trying to slowly leave our family pack in favor of their friends. They want to herd together with other kids of the same age and push away at times from family. Even as the balance of time spent at home or out with friends is changing, keep an eye out for your child's sibling relationships. Encourage him to set aside a little time doing something he and his sibling enjoy. When friends move or change packs, siblings endure.

Watching our children's relationships with one another evolve might be the most joyful and most painful part of parenting. But take heart; kids monitor each other really well. They give honest, if harsh, criticism of poor behavior. They do not hesitate to call each other on cheating, bragging, whining, or nastiness. You do not need to intervene as they teach each other these lessons unless the punishment is genuinely too harsh. Here is the truth: almost all kids will learn these lessons. Your children are learning them at home instead of on the playground and that can be hard to witness. But they are learning them from people who love them (each other) and who have other opportunities to show real empathy toward each other.

So grab your coffee and go into a different room. Or grab a pillow and join in.

39

They're Mean!: Friend Management

We all want our kids to have friends. Friendships teach great skills, and can bring great joy to childhood as well as adulthood. But they also bring great drama. One of the main tasks of growing up is to learn to make, sustain, enjoy, and occasionally end friendships.

One of the main tasks of parenting is to support that learning. But it's hard! Our kids count on us to see the forest for the trees, even if they have a face full of bark and can't see past the pain of ramming into that one huge oak. Whether our child is 2 or 12, our first big decision is, "Should I get involved?"

Let's talk (again) about bullying.

Bullying is normal, but not acceptable. This has gotten our society in a lot of trouble, because for decades the attitude has been, "Aw, they're just being kids." Has anyone seen *The Hunger Games*? They were just kids, too.

Luckily, we have seen a huge societal shift in the past years, and we as a society no longer tolerate bullying. Kids still do it, though, every day. Bullying is using social power to make someone else do what you want him to do. This can be as mild as saying, "If you don't play trucks with me you have to go home." This can be as horrifying as the middle schoolers who systematically insult, punish, and demean another student until that student takes their advice to die.

If you fear your child is being bullied.

This is not the time to take a step back. This is the time to model resilience for your child, rather than giving her an opportunity to find resilience on her own.

1. Know the signs.

   - A sudden change in mood, emotional state, or attitude about going to school

   - Unexplained missing or damaged belongings, or injuries.

   - Change in attitude toward, or big drop off in, social time (in person or via text)

   - Avoiding activities that used to be important to your child

   - Sadness or irritability that persists, or a lot of physical complaints of illness or pain

   - Major change in appetite or sleep

2. Ask, and listen.

3. Don't settle for a nonanswer. If you know something is wrong, be persistent until your child is willing to discuss with you or a trusted adult.

4. Know the laws in your state and rules in your school or community.

5. Go online with your child and find an action plan—stopbullying .gov and other resources exist with lots of help.

6. Listen to your child while you work to empower and protect her. Involving her in the process, even if you eventually need to involve the school or even the police, will help her feel more powerful.

Teach resilience by acknowledging and working to improve the situation.

If you fear your child is bullying someone.

This is also not the time to take a step back. The hardest thing for a parent in this situation is to keep an open mind. Believe me when I tell you that most kids will try bullying. Sometimes they stop because it doesn't work, sometimes because the friend or sibling they try it out on shuts it down. But often, it works! The feeling of getting someone else to do what you want, controlling his actions even for a while, can be very exciting. It is normal to try this, and normal to like it. However, just as it is normal for a two-year-old to do whatever it takes to get her own way, it has to be stopped. Having a child who is bullying doesn't make you a bad parent. Ignoring it, however, is negligent.

1. Know the signs.

    - Your child is getting in trouble at school. Ask the school for more information.

    - Your child's friends never have an opinion different from your child's, and always do what she says.

    - Your child is developing an attitude that he is entitled to whatever he wants from anyone around him.

    - Your child denies responsibility for poor behavior or blames others for problems.

    - You notice unexplained new belongings.

    - Your child's friends are aggressive or mean-spirited.

    - You hear an attitude of exclusivity, or a lot of gossiping with friends.

2. Ask your child about her interactions and behavior, and listen to the answers.

3. Don't accept a nonanswer. Spend more time near your child while he is with peers: drive carpool, get close to the field during sports, or encourage him to have friends to your home where you can observe the interactions.

4. Talk to teachers, coaches, and other parents, and ask about your child's social life.

5. Address bullying.

- Name the behavior as bullying, but don't call your child a bully. Kids know that "a bully" is evil. This is the difference between "You behaved badly" and "You are bad."

- Show empathy for him. Friends are important; it feels good to have others listen to you and do what you want. Leadership is admirable.

- Look for times when your child is being bullied. Often this behavior is learned.

- Be clear in your expectations. Negative or hurtful behavior is not good leadership and won't be tolerated from anyone in your family.

- Require your child to create a list of positive ways to influence his social circle.

- Give consequences that limit his social time when he uses bullying.

- Involve other trusted adults to help you monitor and improve his actions.

Teach resilience by acknowledging and working to improve the situation.

OK, now for all those times that you've determined are *not* bullying.

Most friendships have struggles. As parents, those struggles make us want to jump in to protect our precious children. That, however, often gets in the way of their learning. So, when you can, take one step back.

There is a laundry list of nasty things kids do to each other in the course of friendship:

- Teasing

- Not sharing

- Gossiping

- "Frenemy" behavior (undermining a relationship with rivalry and fake support)

- Fighting

- Negative peer pressure

- Criticizing

Additionally, there are the normal hurt feelings and difficulties that are not at all intentional, and sometimes beyond a child's control: Not being able to invite all your friends to your birthday party. Wanting to spend time alone with someone else, which leaves another child out. New interests or hobbies that alter a child's social circle. The parents' friendships change, which alters who kids spend time with on weekends.

Each of these behaviors may exist within a strong friendship that will outlast the challenge. And any of these can get hurtful enough that your child is better off ending the friendship.

How can we take one step back and let our children navigate these difficult decisions in ways that teach them?

The ground-shipping rule: Wait three business days.

Kids often come home with tales of a hurtful social interaction. Our first instinct as parents is to jump in and do something. Find the child that hurt ours, tell him what a little snot he is, or call his parents and tell them. If you're not worried that your child is being bullied in a repeated fashion, the best thing to do is to wait three days. Three school days. I can't tell you how many times I've heard from a parent, "I was so angry with this other child, I couldn't sleep or stop thinking about it. It was so hard to stay out of it. When I asked my child a couple of days later what was going on? She could hardly even remember what I was talking about!"

Feelings change over time. What feels intense and urgent to a child just after it's happened will often mellow and calm or even turn into a joke between the two kids. Some of the best resilience we teach is by just waiting to see what happens with no intervention.

When your child is hurt.

Your desire to smash that "friend" into a million pieces is totally normal. Before you jump in your car to hunt her down, however, go through this very brief exercise.

1. On a scale of 1 to 10, how upset is your child?

2. On a scale of 1 to 10, how upset are you?

3. If you are more upset than your child, figure out why. You might have a history with this type of friend or interaction. You might have an issue with this other child or with that child's parent. Try to keep your issues separate from your child's concern.

4. Is your child asking for help? If so, what help does he want?

   Often our kids just want to be able to talk about it. They don't need us—or want us—to *do* anything.

When your child does want your help.

This is when we have an opportunity to teach all kinds of resilience (and self-respect, too).

1. **Listen** to the whole story and don't interrupt.

2. **Show empathy** for the feelings your child expresses or demonstrates.

3. **Ask** what she might do now. This shows faith in her problem solving and interest in her next steps. You're focusing on moving through the emotions to taking actions.

4. **Give feedback** only if she asks for it.

5. **Ask her to let you know how it goes.**

6. **Praise her process.** This means focusing on her willingness to communicate a struggle, her ability to express her feelings and her desire to improve the situation. She has control over all of those things.

Friendship deal-breakers.

We want our children to know that some actions are not tolerable. No matter how much we care for someone, there are certain things that person might do that would cause us to end the relationship, and should. Think about your child in 10 or 20 years—don't you need him to know that he has the power and the right to get out of a painful relationship?

A great way to make that point is to talk theoretically. Next time you're at dinner with a child who is eight or older, ask: "What would someone have to do for you to stop being friends with him or her?" This is a great exercise, because it plants the idea that we don't tolerate everything for the sake of friendship, or even love.

If your older elementary child or tween is in a friendship that you feel is toxic, you need to get involved. You will build more resilience if you can help your child realize that for herself, but the lesson is important either way. Show empathy for the pain involved, but do your best—and engage other adults your child loves—to guide her toward the self-respect necessary to end a hurtful relationship. This process can take a long time, so stay involved.

Friendships are important to our children. Even if they don't keep these friends into adulthood, they will keep the lessons they learn about friendship for life.

40

They're Strict!: Teacher Management

School is a place to learn a lot of resilience. Even better, it is a place filled with child development experts with years of practice teaching children to be resilient. Most often, the best thing parents can do is to get out of the way of those lessons.

Not always, of course. You may be fuming, thinking of a situation you experienced or know of when a teacher did not have a child's best interest in mind and/or a school disregarded the child's needs. In those situations, we need to (just as in any bullying situation) stand with or in front of our child. If you believe your child is being victimized or harmed in a way that will have lasting effects, get in and talk to those educators. Speak up and make sure you're heard.

Most often, though, our kids face challenges at school that they can handle. Challenges that will teach them. That will benefit our kids as they grow, if we are able to take one step back.

The school day itself teaches the pre-k to eighth-grade student a great number of skills needed to be resilient.

Wake-up and get ready.

It takes perseverance to go to school, especially because most kids (and adults) don't want to.

- Kids can learn to get up when awoken (or from an alarm clock starting around fourth grade) and to go through their morning tasks in time for breakfast and school.

- Parents should encourage this responsibility, and not rearrange their own schedules repeatedly to accommodate kids who constantly run behind.

- If kids get in trouble at school and home for being late, they will be more motivated to get up and moving.

Walk into school with homework and belongings.

These are the child's responsibility, not ours. Driving a forgotten piece of homework or band instrument to school once is a kindness. Doing it over and over again will teach your child that he will always be rescued, not that he needs to be resilient.

- Even young children learn the patterns teachers have in place to put backpacks in lockers, notes in the bin, and homework in the basket.

- Parents can encourage our kids to find systems that work and change bad habits. We should not make excuses when our kids lose things, but search out the reasons and encourage that child to problem solve. Speaking as someone who would lose her head if it wasn't attached, that doesn't change in adulthood. Help your child find ways around her forgetfulness or distractibility or even ADD, so that she can be resilient in spite of any challenges she has.

- When kids see grades dropping because of forgotten homework or equipment, they will see that solutions need to be found.

Following rules.

Some rules seem dumb, or pointless, or arbitrary, and some are all of these things. School teaches the skill of following rules, which is an important skill in adulthood.

- Kids actually like rules. They use and enforce them in games, and life, all the time. Teachers need rules and our kids need to learn to follow them, even if the kids don't understand the purpose of a rule. When our children are grown we want them to question rules, but elementary school is rarely the right time to learn that skill.

• Parents need to support the school and its rules. I'm not just saying that because my mom was a teacher. If we don't agree with the authority of our child's school, we put our kids in a very bad spot. They can't be expected to follow school rules 35 hours each week if we undermine those rules. This is almost as difficult for kids as having two parents in the same home ignore each others' rules. The child does not know what to do!

Struggling with a new concept.

Hopefully our kids will struggle with their schoolwork. First of all, that means that they are learning. If it all comes easy, they could be going further. Second, facing challenges in school teaches kids the work needed to overcome those challenges.

• Kids can and should speak up when they don't understand something. Doing so can be hard. It takes courage to speak up, or to go get help.

• Parents support kids by noticing when something is hard. Keeping an eye on grades, going through the papers that come home, and asking your child about the easiest and hardest thing she learned that day are all ways to be clued in to obstacles.

• If an obstacle exists, don't jump in. Ask, "How do you think you could learn more about that?" and take one step back. Whatever solution your child finds, let him or her try that one out first. If there is no success, then help her brainstorm more options.

Not understanding an assignment.

There is a great lesson to be learned when a child doesn't understand a project or homework. Don't let your child use this as an excuse to give up. This is a chance to practice problem solving and perseverance.

Ask your child who else might know, or how to get in touch with a classmate or a teacher. If the problem can't get solved tonight, what will she do in the morning at school to get her question answered?

Speaking up against injustice.

Sometimes adults get it wrong. Learning to recognize the importance of standing up for yourself or someone else builds resilience.

- Kids can figure out who to talk to when someone in authority doesn't have the whole story or has made an unfair decision. They may need guidance about how to approach the adult respectfully, or where to go if that avenue doesn't work.

- Parents benefit kids by giving them support and honesty. Some rules or consequences may frustrate a child but are actually necessary for the greater good. Taking one step back while a child tries to right an injustice proves that we support and respect our child, even though we can't (and shouldn't) control the outcome.

Getting in trouble.

Just about every child gets in trouble at school at some point. There is so much to learn from facing a consequence at school that will build a child's resilience.

- **Community.** Being a part of a group involves rules.

- **Accountability.** Actions have consequences.

- **Fellowship.** Getting in trouble with friends teaches a lot about the friendship.

- **Honesty.** Most principals will give a much harsher punishment for a child who tries to lie his way out of trouble than one who stands up and admits the wrongdoing.

- **Survival.** Getting in trouble is hard. Making it through the punishment teaches its own lessons.

• **Reconciliation.** After the punishment is over, things go back to business as usual. This gives a child the opportunity to improve her behavior and try again to be the person she most wants to be.

Whether or not you agree to the trouble-in-school-means-trouble-at-home rule, don't intervene in the consequences at school unless you see real danger. Our children can live through discomfort, embarrassment, boredom, and difficulty. They need to learn that they can by doing it. That means real resilience.

41

They're Unfair!: Coach/Instructor Management

Your child is signed up for a team, a sport, or a lesson. Great! Assuming you are not raising the next Olympic athlete or child protégé, you had a lot of other reasons for encouraging or allowing her to sign up. Your child has more to learn from that instructor than just the sport or skill.

Here are some of the most common challenges kids face, and how to use these struggles to build resilience.

She changed her mind.

An activity seemed like a great idea at sign-up time, but now she doesn't want to go. Or it was fun the first couple of times but now she wants to quit. For children and tweens, it's usually worth finishing out the season or session and not signing up for that again. This demonstrates a good blend of perseverance and compassion. About 10 percent of the time there is a great reason to quit in the middle. When that happens, teach your child to quit responsibly. Give notice to the teacher, and have older children apologize to teammates without having to explain themselves.

He doesn't like it but you feel it's important.

In our family, everyone takes swimming lessons until he is an independent swimmer. No discussion, no argument. We believe this is a safety issue. Kids take required classes all day long at school, so this is not a new concept. You may have a skill that you find nonnegotiable outside of academics, like a religious class or a musical instrument, or some kind of physical activity. It is alright to enforce one or two of these. Your child can be resilient enough to handle it.

Overscheduling.

Too many activities can crush a child's resilience. With no breathing room, no space for boredom or creativity, there is no opportunity for decision making and much less time for learning life's bigger lessons. If you can't figure out what your child should do less of or stop, ask him. Make sure that your child's schedule reflects your family's priorities.

- Do you put family time first? That means a schedule with some completely free hours each week for hanging out together, and a meal together most days.

- Do you value self-care? Then make sure her schedule has time for sit-down meals, enough sleep, and some relaxation.

- Is education important? Demonstrate that by prioritizing homework time over other activities.

Not making the team.

This is both painful and educational. If your child doesn't get an opportunity that he tried out for, show empathy. If his frustration persists, ask him to problem solve. What does he want to accomplish and what might help him achieve it? Does he need more practice, better skills, or a new goal? This will not be the only time in life that he falls short of a goal. Help him work through the emotion to meaningful action.

Sitting on the bench.

Sometimes players sit on the bench. Even great players, hardworking players, dedicated players have to watch while others play. Don't jump in. If there is a conversation to be had, the first one is between your child and her coach.

"What can I do to get off the bench, coach?"

Sometimes the answer will be instructive: "Show up to practice on time. Be a better listener. Pass more to your teammates." Sometimes it will be arbitrary: "Wait." Occasionally it will be impossible. One of my sons asked this of his football coach and the answer was, "Grow." This might happen in the school musical or a dance recital as well; anytime our kids take roles as a part of a group, they may experience feeling sidelined.

Advise them to advocate for themselves. Be supportive, but take a step back. They will survive, and learn.

Losing.

This is when empathy just kills us parents. We have no control over the outcome of a game or competition but we try to will ourselves into the moment. We yell ourselves hoarse, coach from the sidelines, and sometimes embarrass ourselves and our kids. So what to do?

1. Get yourself under control. Take that one step back and remember that this is your child's competition, not yours.

2. Keep in mind the bigger purpose of this activity. You wanted your child to learn, right? Losing teaches a lot more than winning.

3. Put your child's effort and character at the forefront of your mind. He may focus on the loss, but you can focus on the growth.

4. Stop coaching from the sidelines, unless you're the coach.

Getting in trouble.

Just like with school, there is a lot to learn when a child gets in trouble with a coach or an instructor. Don't stand between your child and that challenge. If he was supposed to practice piano and didn't, then that happened and has consequences. If she talked back to the director? That happened too, and should have consequences.

We don't have to be the only adult in our child's life who is helping him learn resilience. In fact, this might be the greatest gift a coach or instructor can give.

42

Somebody Has a Girlfriend: Relationship Management

A good friend of mine told me, long before we ever had kids, "I'm not letting my kids have boyfriends or girlfriends until high school at the earliest!" That made total sense to me at the time. Like so many things I thought I could control, I have learned an important lesson here.

We can guide our kids' behavior, but not their emotions. Preschoolers, and sometimes even toddlers, begin by playing House, or Family. So cute! And so completely normal. My son came home from his four-year-old preschool class one day to say, "I'm somebody's boyfriend." What? "Yup, she told me."

Think back, ladies. Chinese-fortune-teller paper origami things that we scrawled boys' names into, school bus rides on field trips, whispered conversations at sleepovers. The idea of partnering up is on kids' (especially girls') minds from a young age. And boys are not immune. Just as our children do with jobs—playing teacher or firefighter or astronaut—they are experimenting with what they want to be as an adult. Most of us do want our kids to grow up and find a great partner.

Instead of forbidding these conversations, we can use them to teach our children, and guide them toward finding that great partner, and treating her or him well. Also, as we all know, having a life partner requires resilience.

Parents are the best sex-ed teachers in a child's life. The conversations we have with our kids about sex begin as soon as they notice the differences between girls and boys. Start young and establish a pattern:

- **Welcome.** Be glad your child is asking you and not a friend or sibling. Make it clear that you are always a safe person to ask. There is no shame in asking a question.

- **Thoughtfulness.** Consider the age and personality of the child in front of you. What is the child really asking and how much information is she ready to learn?

- **Honesty.** You may choose not to answer a child's question yet, or give every bit of information you have, but do not lie.

- **Clarity.** Give useful amounts of information in language your child understands. If you use a word he doesn't know, give him or help him find the definition. It's OK to give a very short answer. If your child wants more, you'll hear a follow-up question.

- **Value.** Think about the lesson you want your child to take in along with the facts. That message might be about modesty, or pride, or privacy, or something else. You are the best person to pass on your family's values.

- **Repetition.** Important messages bear repeating. Let your child know, each time you have an important conversation, that you'll discuss it again.

ASK◦DOCTOR G

Parent Q: What is normal sexual interest in a child and when should I worry?

*I*f you see a big change in a child's level of interest in romantic or sexual ideas, take a more serious look. When children are being sexually molested (by anyone, even an older child), some children will increase sexual behavior, and embrace a much more adult persona. Step in quickly to protect that child and seek out help.

Toddlers.

"Boy" and "girl" friends this age are all friends. Steer little ones away from this kind of more mature language, and encourage them to be kind and caring toward all their friends.

> **Sex-ed at this age.** Two-and three-year-olds are still learning that their parents' bodies are separate from their own. Start excellent respect and habits early by teaching children to ask permission before touching private areas and before kissing someone. Many parents end up uncomfortably pushing their child's hands away from genitals, but it's stronger to address the issue directly: "This is a private area, you need to ask if it's OK to touch me there."

Toddlers are busy learning to name things. Even if you use a made-up name for genitals, make sure she knows the real words, too. Words have power, and show that we don't need to feel shame about facts ... even if that does lead your child to announce to his preschool class how sorry he feels for his mommy because she "doesn't get a penis!" Ahem.

Preschoolers.

Playing wedding, house, or family is all part of a child's way of working out what he or she thinks and knows about relationships of many kinds. Watch your child play for a while, and address any activities you think are not appropriate. Kids should not:

• Share a bed when they're playing that they are grown-ups.

• Practice kissing or adult hugging.

• Pretend to smoke, or drink alcohol, or use drugs.

This establishes your future expectations. You are not telling your child how to feel, but you are setting boundaries on how he behaves.

Watching a child's imaginary play will let you know a lot about what that child is learning and growing to believe. If you're worried about what you see, that is a great time to step in.

➢ **Sex-ed at this age.** Kids this age touch themselves, a lot! Start the privacy conversation by explaining that this is something to do only when you're by yourself, in your room. This is a totally normal behavior, but a private one.

Four- and five-year-olds may have some questions about babies. As they see pregnant women, they may ask for some specifics about how the baby gets out, or even how the baby gets in. Remember that you can fall back on the previous structure, answering in small bits, and waiting for follow-up questions, if any come. At this age they often don't. A friend of mine always answers this first "Where do babies come from" question with, "From the hospital, honey." She says it buys her about six months.

Ages 5–7.

Most children this age continue to express their thoughts about romance and sex in pretend play, but kids who are slightly more worldly may begin claiming "real" relationships. If your first-grader comes home with a new heartthrob, ask about behaviors: "What do you do together?" Chances are, this is a relationship in name only. Again, focus on behaviors as what you need to guide. As for emotions, show empathy and listen, without getting enmeshed in the playground gossip scene.

➢ **Sex-ed at this age.** Keep reinforcing the message that your child has control over his or her own body. Areas that are covered by bathing suits are private, and kids should not touch other people in those spots, or let themselves be touched in those spots. The only possible exceptions are parents, and during a doctor's visit.

In some communities, it is time for kids to have the basic facts about how the baby actually gets in there. For some kids, it is way too soon. The main goal here is to get to your kids before their peers do. This is because their friends are likely to mislead them, scare them, and make them feel dumb for not knowing. Whatever you might choose to tell an early elementary schooler about puberty, or sex, or any "adult" topic, be clear about keeping this information private. You do not want to be the parent of the child who goes on to teach every other child in third grade about this topic.

Ages 8–10.

This is the age when kids often stop playing with children of the opposite sex. There is a lot of social pressure to stop being friends with kids of the other gender, and that can be really painful for children who have had a great friend up until now but feel that relationship dissolving. You may or may not be able to help the kids involved overcome this obstacle. Communicating with the other child's family may help.

For kids who have their own cell phone or are spending time in co-ed groups for unstructured "hang out" time, the urge to pair up can be great. Ask your child about this. Listen to her emotions and continue to make your expectations about her behaviors clear.

As gender roles and "rules" become stronger, kids will also start to be fascinated by the idea of homosexuality. "That's so gay!" can sadly still be heard on many elementary school playgrounds. If you hear your child use that word as an insult, talk about it. I very much hope that you will create a home where everyone is welcome and no one may be insulted for what orientation he or she is. But, whatever your moral stance on homosexuality, be sure to pass on your values about not bullying at the same time.

> Sex-ed at this age. Whatever you have or haven't told your child by now, her friends are very likely weighing in with their own ideas (and values). It's time to let your child know that you are the expert, and she can check in with anything she's heard or any questions she has. Continue to reinforce your values of safety, and good communication.

Ages 11–12.

Some kids this age create relationships. A "relationship" may never exist outside of text messaging, but, to the tweens involved, it doesn't feel any less real or important. We can and should guide our children's behavior, but we will have no success if we try to tell them what they feel: "You don't love him." "This isn't real!" Denying your child's emotions will only serve to close down communication between you and the child, giving you less chance to teach anything.

Playing with these relationships can teach good lessons. In a middle schooler's life, a romance is usually exciting, but secondary to friendships. Great news! When that relationship ends, and it will, your child will learn to get through the sadness or anger and go back to focusing on friends and family. That is a great life lesson.

It may be time to start thinking about dating rules. Is your child allowed to be alone with someone if she is "going out?" How much supervision does your tween need if there will be a co-ed group at an outing or party or event? All kids are fascinated with the idea of acting older than they are. Sexual exploration is a terrible place to experiment.

Be careful not to get enmeshed. We know our kids' friends pretty well, and it is easy to get invested in their romances. Don't do it! Your child needs to know that you are 100 percent on his "side." Whatever happens, however and whenever this relationship ends, your tween will not benefit from having to consider your emotions with his. Keep your focus on his behavior.

➤ **Sex-ed at this age.** Most schools are starting to address the issue of sex education in the classroom setting around this age. Find out what they're covering and get knowledgeable yourself. Ask your child what he heard, and what he learned or believes about it. Learn slang terms from your child, and keep gently pushing these values: respect, privacy, pride, caution, safety.

As our kids head into the teen years, there is one thing we know for sure: We will not be with them when they make these big decisions. The best we can hope for is that they hear our voices in their heads.

43

Take a Chance

I want my kids to take risks: to climb trees, to join a new team, to raise their hands in class when they're not sure they're right. My kids need to try a new skill or say hello to a person who looks different than anyone they've ever met. My children must experience a new food, a new activity, a new idea.

Everyone who talks about parenting says, "We can't just tell our kids to do something, we have to do it, too." Absolute truth. Want your kids to exercise? Go run. Want your kids to sit through church? Sit next to them.

Risk-taking is even harder. We can't just take our own chances and model that courage. We must take risks with our children. Not only take risks near, or next to, or in conjunction with our kids—we must actually risk our children. What?

I'm not asking you to foolishly risk your child's life.

I'm saying that our kids need to have the experience of taking risks. They need to see our faith in them. Think about the very many times we say to our children, "Be careful!" Parents are all about caution. If you are raising a natural born risk-taker, then your caution is appropriate. You have a child who is naturally resilient, who needs no encouragement or reminder that she can try, leap, succeed, or fail.

For the rest of us, we need to finish the sentence. Our kids need to hear, "Be careful, but try." Play that game, go on that outing, go one step further than your comfort zone.

No one learns resilience in her comfort zone. No one learns much of anything at all in her comfort zone.

In order to actively teach resilience—without intentionally putting our kids in harms' way—there are two important issues to tackle:

1. How can we get our hesitant kids to take a little more risk?

2. How can cautious parents motivate themselves to risk a little more?

Moving kids out of their comfort zone.

Toddlers.

We move two- and three-year-olds out of their comfort zone every time we ask them to stray from the routine. Trying new foods, flexing a nap time, even putting a coat on before shoes can stress a routine-oriented toddler.

➢ Encourage resilience by offering choices. "I'm not able to take you home before these errands, but you can choose—should we go to the bank first, or the store?" Kids love autonomy (the independence to make choices), and this is a crucial step in building resilience.

Preschoolers.

Extend this strategy with four- and five-year-olds.

➢ Encourage your little one to try something new, like asking a new adult a question. Give him some autonomy about the setting, or the question, or how he approaches the situation. Make the task and the reason clear and then leave the rest of the decision making in his hands.

Ages 5–7.

Focus on moments that your child finds to be a challenge.

➢ Since resilience requires problem solving, ask your early elementary schooler how many options she sees that might overcome the challenge she faces. If she and a friend can't find anything fun to do, ask them to list ways to attack that issue. Do something they've done before, look online for a list of fun rainy day activities for six-year-old girls (oh yes, there are some), go through your list of chores, let her little brother decide.... Whatever they choose and try, that's resilience!

Ages 8–10.

Shift from problem solving to problem finding.

➢ When we push a child to do something that makes him uncomfortable, he pushes back. So ask him to find the problem with taking that risk. This is a great skill, since it teaches critical thinking and planning. Moreover, he will learn to respond to caution with questions: "Should I be careful here? What am I concerned might happen? Is that actually likely?"

Ages 11–12.

We worry so much about negative peer pressure in middle school. As parents, we know that our kids will face pressure, external or internal, to try new activities. Some of those activities, such as substance use, bullying, and skipping school, are terrible ideas! Some, such as trying out for the school play, joining a youth group, or taking a new class, are great.

➢ Talk to kids this age about evaluating risk instead of avoiding it.

Autonomy leads to problem solving. When we encourage our kids to be responsible for achieving a goal, but leave the path mostly up to them, they learn how to accomplish something. More importantly, they learn that they CAN accomplish that something.

Moving parents out of our comfort zones.

From an audience of 500, a very frustrated father asked me, "Am I supposed to protect my kids or teach them to be resilient?" The answer, of course, is, "Both." That struggle is the very essence of parenting. It seems like a contradiction, right?

The first couple of years of our kids' lives are all about protection. At first, these little beings are totally helpless and need everything from adults: food, protection, even carrying them from place to place. Then they start to move, getting to what my husband calls the all-legs-and-no-brains age, where we have to defend them constantly from their environment. A psychiatrist friend of mine calls this age Suicide Watch. As a mom who has performed a flying tackle to stop my 17-month-old from sticking the car key into an outlet, and pulled another child off the teetering top of a radiator(!), I might have to agree.

Soon, however, we have to stop standing between our kids and the world. We need to take that one crucial step back and let them learn, try, fall, and learn about getting back up. The biggest challenge for parents is to manage the thought shift necessary to focus on the goal of learning rather than the goal of safety.

Risks are the key. Giving our kids the opportunity, and sometimes the nudge, to learn how to find, weigh, and take risks will give them all the skills they need to protect themselves.

The most popular seminar I give is called "Teach Kids to Make the World a Better Place." Over and over again, parents cite this as their fondest hope and dream for their children. Nobody ever made the world a better place without taking some risks.

44

Bad Things Happen

A patient of mine said to me one day, "I'm really sad because my dad is dying of cancer." We talked about it a while—the stresses, the near future tragedy, the joys of her past relationship with him. Just before she left, she cautioned me, "Don't mention this to my daughter, she doesn't know." Her 11-year-old is also my patient, and was due in to see me the following week.

The next week came, and I saw the 11-year-old. At some point in the visit I asked Mom to leave, like I always do, so I can have a few minutes alone with a tween patient. This is great practice for kids, as they learn to talk to a doctor for themselves. When we were by ourselves I asked, "How are things?" "Awful," she said. "My grandpa is dying of cancer. But don't say anything to my mom, I'm not sure she knows."

When we "protect" children from scary or sad news, we often just deny them and ourselves a chance to have really meaningful conversations.

As I've said before, we can't protect kids from difficulty. So it's our job to help them learn how to handle bad news instead. Our kids can learn about tragedy with a message of helplessness or a message of resilience. The silver lining of every family illness or stressor is the chance to teach our kids how strong they are.

Before bad news hits, prepare!

Before difficulty comes their way, start preparing your kids for strength and resilience with a Coping List. This is a (hopefully long) list of all the healthy ways your child can think of to make herself feel better when she is sad or scared. This exercise builds resilience in any situation (like a rained out event or missed playdate), but is especially helpful in the face of prolonged trouble.

You and your child will know best what relieves her stress. Here are a few age-appropriate suggestions to get you started:

Toddlers.

➢ Holding a favorite lovey or stuffed animal

➢ Singing a song

➢ Playing tag

Preschoolers.

➢ Hugging a person

➢ Dancing or jumping

➢ Sharing jokes

Ages 5–7.

➢ Creating a picture

➢ Reading a particular book

➢ Taking a bike ride

Ages 8–10.

➢ Playing a sport

➢ Writing in a journal

➢ Sitting in a particular spot

Ages 11–12.

➢ Talking to a friend

➢ Listening to music

➢ Playing a game

The longer this list, the better for everyone to know there are options. For good health, steer away from food as comfort, even though it certainly is.

Which bad news should we tell them?

If a stressor affects your family directly and will be long term, your kids need to hear about it from you. This might be a move, an illness, an injury, a deployment or other separation, a death, or any other major event that will disrupt the emotional balance or routine of your home for more than a day or two.

ASK DOCTOR G

Parent Q: This most recent school shooting was on the other side of the country. My husband thinks we should talk to the kids about it, but they are just six and three. Isn't that too young?

*I*f a tragedy happens in the news, and your child is less than eight years old, it is quite possible you do not need to share the information. If the ripples will rock your family in any way, then you may need to give a little information to your younger child. For kids eight and older, they are likely to hear about the event outside your home or through the media. Use this opportunity to start to talk to them about how to react when tragedy strikes strangers.

Why should we tell them? Three reasons.

1. To give our kids a solid foundation, we need their trust. Sharing bad news is an opportunity to earn that trust. We are the people who will tell the truth, or explain why we're not ready to talk about something yet.

2. The people who are caring for kids ages 12 and under need to be the go-to experts about pretty much everything. It doesn't help kids to make them guess why all the adults are sad or angry, or why nothing feels normal. We are the people our kids can count on to have the information they need, or help them find that information.

3. This is our chance to focus on a child's personality and needs. The person sharing bad news has the opportunity to teach a little. Frame the conversation with the values we want to teach that child. We are in charge, and our children can rely on us to take that responsibility seriously.

When should we tell them?

As adults, we will be more successful talking to kids after we've had a chance to process our own emotions, if at all possible. That first rush of feelings may very well scare our children, who operate more on empathy than logical understanding of events. Just as our kids tend to laugh if we laugh, they often cry if we cry, and are terrified when they see our fear. If it's possible, adults should lean on friends or adult family to get their own reaction under control before explaining to kids what is happening. That will better allow us to focus on the child and the conversation.

What should we tell them?

Kids do not need every detail. Just like with our conversations about sex, we can be honest with children without giving them every bit of information we know. Start with a short sentence, the most important thing you need your child to hear. Some kids will ask a question, some will have a reaction, some will change the subject. Any of those reactions might be developmentally normal, at any age. Adults do the same thing!

So, how exactly?

1. **Give the news in one sentence.** Too much prep will likely stress him out, and you won't be sure what he was able to hear and really take in.

2. **Answer the questions he asks.** Don't give more information than he asks for; he will ask for more when he is ready.

3. **Ask how he feels.** Listen to the answers without trying to change his mind or "fix" it. We can't control our kids' emotions, and we don't help them to be resilient when we try. Resilience comes along with hard feelings, not instead of them.

4. **Validate his feelings.** Use his actual words. "I hear that you are terrified." "I understand that you wish this wasn't happening." "You don't know what to do."

5. **Remind him of his coping list.** This emphasizes his strengths. The point here is not to cry, but rather to express those emotions and then find a way to work through those hard feelings, and possibly have some good feelings as well.

6. **Plan another time to talk.** Make sure he knows you'll check back in about this, and get more information as it becomes important.

When trouble occurs to, in, or near your family, recognize the opportunity. Our kids listen to what we say, and they watch what we do. Building strong kids requires finding our own strength and resilience. Only then can they learn that we get through hard times, and learn to find the positive again. That is resilience.

45

Failure Builds Success

The only thing that scares most parents more than our own failure is the idea of our kids failing. We want to shield them from that pain, from humiliation, from what must surely be the devastating consequences to their self-esteem if they fail. Because of all that love and empathy, we ignore what we know to be true.

Failure is great for kids.

Failing teaches. Perseverance, humor, empathy, determination; there is no end to what a person can learn when he fails at something. Our job, as parents, is not to protect our kids from failing. Our job is to let them fail and then help them learn from that experience.

It absolutely hurts to watch a child suffer. Suck it up.

You know how to do this. Your child learned to walk, and that involved letting him try, and fall, and try, and fall, over and over again. You encouraged your child to walk when you were pretty sure he couldn't do it, that he would fall on his diapered butt and look at you like "Why'd ya do that?" You knew he had to learn.

Take that pattern, and apply it to math. Think about it when your child is learning friendship, communication, or sports. Instead of finding ways to help your child succeed, remember that your job is to encourage her to try: "Come on honey, just one step."

I ask audiences, "Why not let your child fail?" The answers swirl around, but in the end they all fit in two categories:

1. If she fails, I fail.

2. If I let her fail, she'll hate me.

Please understand, I have these same fears. When my son is doing badly at something, ruins a friendship, or causes a problem at school, my ego is on the line. It takes a lot of work to remind myself that I can't take ownership of his choices, his emotions, his life. If I don't step in to save my child from a mistake, or rescue him by telling him exactly what to do, when he knows I could, I risk his wrath. All of these feel like excellent reasons to just fix whatever the problem is.

I have to keep my eye on the goal. The true goal is to raise kids who can fix their own problems. It doesn't surprise me that my nine-year-old turns to me for The Answer. I do not want my 29-year-old to have to turn to me with his problems, except to tell me what he did and how it turned out.

In this way, problem solving is no different than laundry. If I do it for my kids their entire childhood, they will not know how to do it for themselves as adults.

We have to change how we think. Our kids' successes are not the touchdowns of parenting. Our kids' failures? Now those are the opportunities. Imagine this Holiday Letter:

Dear Friends,

We hope you are enjoying a magical holiday season! We just wanted to take a minute to tell you about the wonderful things that have happened in our family this year.

Susie failed math first trimester! She tried flashcards and a study group, but that was no help. She called the homework help line, and sometimes it was useful, but she just didn't have the study skills to translate that to the test. Next she asked for a tutor, and they meet after school twice a week. She's remediating fractions, and getting stronger with her math facts. She's hoping for a C this trimester. We're really proud!

Jason didn't make the soccer varsity. He was on varsity last year, so imagine our surprise! He's come to realize that he should have gone to the summer drill sessions that were offered, and has decided to do them this year in hopes of getting back on the team next year ....

I don't imagine I'll see too many of these in my mailbox, but these are the real triumphs of parenting. If you're wondering: We don't send a holiday letter. We cheat by just sending pictures. Kids learn a lot more when things don't go their way than when everything is smooth sailing. The hard work for us is allowing the failure to happen, and coaching them to take in the lessons afterwards. Praising resilience after failure does not always feel as rewarding to us as praising a success. Learning that resilience, however, IS a huge success.

Don't rob your kids of the learning failure will bring them.

PART IV

MAKING CHANGE HAPPEN

HOW TO ACTUALLY GET KIDS TO *DO* THIS STUFF

46

Can Your Kids Count on You?

So, how do we get kids to DO all this great stuff? Finally: The "how!"

Are you frustrated? "These ideas sound great," you may be thinking, "but how in the world can I get my child to actually do any of this?" That is what this section is for. Like I told you in the Introduction, I waited until this point in the book to talk about "how" because it's often not any fun to do. But it is so totally worth the struggle.

You've thought about all this before: How do I get my kids to do what they need to do, to be respectful and responsible? Is it OK to yell? What about when they ignore me? How much should we try to be "fair" and why do they always say we're not? Why won't they just listen???

I have struggled with all these questions. I have gotten to meet thousands of families. Everyone struggles with discipline.

Discipline: "Training to act in accordance with rules," according to the dictionary.

For some readers, this section is an affirmation or a reminder. A cheering section that says, "You know how to do this, keep it up!" Very few if any of these ideas are brand new. But see if the following chapters can encourage you to persevere, and renew your energy to do your parent work.

Most of us can't change our kids by just telling them to change. Remember when you held your adorable baby, trying to get her to sleep when she didn't want to, or eat something he had decided not to eat? I will remind you of what you've known since then. You can't change your child's behavior. Only your child can change her behavior. But here is the good news (and the secret kids would vehemently deny): children's behavior is fairly predictable. So all you have to do is change how *you* respond to your child's words and behavior. Your change will lead to their change.

So basically you may have to do the second hardest thing in the world: change your own behavior. The good news is you've got lots of options. Read on and find a fit for your family, your philosophy, your child, and you. These principles are a guide that can work in a huge number of situations. I challenge you to try some. It's not fattening, and it might actually help.

Will your child resist? Oh brother, will he! Life is much more fun for a child who can choose when to listen and decide whether or not she is in the mood to follow the rules. Resistance to these ideas is good news. Resistance means your child has noticed the change and is changing her behavior in response. Persist with your good changes and you will see some of her own. Depending on the child, and on her age when you start to demonstrate your new responses, this change can be really slow. Slow change means your child does not yet believe that this new response is going to stick. Most four- or five-year-olds will change their reactions in a few days. A tween may take months to stop testing the new order and start to believe that you mean what you say. Be strong. If you're not in charge, then (gulp) your child is.

Since you're here in this section, you have a behavior in mind you'd like to change. As my husband is fond of pointing out, people don't like to change. Kids are no exception. If you see a problem, or something that could be better, chances are good that your kids do not share that view. Lucky for you, you're in charge. Yes, you.

Be trustworthy.

Picture this future moment: Your child is a teen. At 15 he is at an after-the-game party and he realizes his ride home is drinking steadily. He knows you've told him that he can always call for a ride, no questions asked. Do you want him to believe you, and call? Or he might think, "They *said* that, but I doubt they *meant* it." How can you jump into the future and convince your son to call? By giving him a time-out today.

I know this is a strange leap to make, but it's how kids' brains work. Every time a child faces a behavior decision, if he thinks about it at all, he will wonder: "If I do _____ what will my parents really do?" Your job is to teach your child that you will do what you said, every time. You need to be the most trustworthy person in his entire life.

- "If you speak to me that way one more time, we're going home."
- "If you hit, I will not play with you."
- "If you don't do as I said, you have to sit on the bench."
- "If you get off that bench, you're going to your room."
- "If you come out of your room again, I'll cancel your birthday party."

Make sure your threats are promises and keep your promises. Every time. When you give the consequence you said, you are teaching your child, "You can count on me."

What about the great promises? Keep them!

- "I'll be there for the spelling bee."
- "I'm coming up to read you a story."
- "I'll play with you when I'm done on the phone."
- "You'll see me before bedtime, or I'll call if there's a delay."
- "I love you no matter what."

ASK DOCTOR G

Parent Q: I often threaten something but then back down because it seems too harsh. How can I teach my son to listen without being mean?

Many parents tell me that they back off a promised consequence because they can't stand to hurt their child that way. If, in your moments of frustration, you make threats that are huge or unreasonable, do a little preparation. Make yourself a list of reasonable consequences that will still make an impression on your son. That way you won't grope for

(continued)

ASK DOCTOR G

(continued)

a punishment and say something you are later unwilling to implement. When you enforce a consequence, you are not showing your child "I'm mean." You are proving to your child that he can trust you, no matter what.

Be in charge.

Every organization needs structure. Your family needs the adult(s) to run the place. The kind of organization you run is up to you, but it needs a few key elements.

1. **Good adult communication.** Whatever decisions you make about numbers 2–5 on this list, your family will struggle if the adults can't agree on who is in charge of what, and how problems are resolved. The adult communication, whether it is parent-to-parent, parent-to-babysitter, or parent-to-grandparent, lets kids know that their foundation is solid and all the adults are talking together about what goes on.

2. **A clear structure.** In my house, whichever parent is home has the final say, but we may choose to wait on a decision until we've had time to discuss it. What one parent says, goes. There is no "I didn't like that answer so I'll just wait and ask Dad." Some families put older siblings in charge of younger ones, and other families treat each child equally. Either way can work, but kids need to know what to expect.

3. **Rules.** A lot of them are needed, in fact. Rules make the foundation of a family more solid. The details are less important than having clear rules themselves. What's so great about rules? Kids need to learn these three elements to manage their behavior.

    a. **Clear expectations.**

    b. **Boundaries.**

    c. **Consistency.**

4. **Consequences.** This is how kids get motivated to continue or change what they're doing. They get the consequence they like

or a consequence they don't, and that guides future behavior. Sounds simple, right? Ha!

5. **Support.** Love, communication, understanding, expectations; all of these sustain kids so that they know that home is a predictable, safe place.

Be confident.

Your kids will love you. They will not always like you, and they will not always thank you or be able to explain your value. But they will love you. So don't hold back on what they need. Don't hesitate to guide behavior for fear of upsetting your child. To change a behavior, we have to get out of our comfort zone.

I'm the parenting expert on the four kids who live with me. *You* are the parenting expert on the kids in your home. Please don't doubt how well you know your children. Don't doubt how much they need you, and that your guidance is the best, most powerful force in their lives.

Kids need to know that the structure isn't going to change. No matter what happens, no matter what they say, how they negotiate with us, how many times they ask, or how they try to get around it, parents are a constant. Parental love, parental guidance, and parental boundaries are equally necessary.

1. You make a rule.

2. Your child breaks the rule.

3. You warn of the consequence.

4. Your child breaks the rule again.

5. You give the consequence.

6. Your child pitches a huge fit.

7. You enforce the consequence anyway.

Your child can count on you.

Patterns teach our children. It only takes thousands of times for them to learn.

47

How to Avoid Being the Parent You Hate

We all have at least one thing about our parenting styles that we would like to never do again. What's your "thing?" Think about your behavior when you are pushed to the edge. What makes your child scared or angry or hurt so that he cannot hear what you are trying to teach him?

In this chapter, you have some homework. First, figure out what defines "the parent you hate." Most often, parents tell me they hate screaming at their kids, and I understand that—it is a loss of control and really awful things can come out of your mouth. Other parents say they berate their kids by calling them "bad" or using other insulting words. Some parents throw things in their most frustrated moments and others completely give in to their children despite their better judgment.

Losing it.

This is the moment when your own behavior gets out of control. A child has angered you, hurt you, or ignored you, or hurt another child. Or perhaps something difficult has happened to you, like you lost your job or have a parent in the hospital or just discovered your checking account is overdrawn, and your child chooses that moment to tell you dinner "sucked." Whatever the cause, you find yourself completely out of control, doing and saying things you don't want to, but can't stop.

I would like to have a magic answer for you (and for myself). There is no off switch that works for every person. In that moment, try to give yourself a "time-out." Break the pattern by closing your eyes or counting to 50 or saying, "We will talk about this in five minutes (or five hours)." Walk away if your children are old enough to be in the room without you. You need to learn what will give you time to bleed the adrenaline from your system so that you can actually teach a lesson. When you are in fight-or-flight mode with your heart pounding and a scream building in your chest, your child may watch you in fascination and horror; however, he or she usually can't really understand what you are yelling.

This skill of recognizing when you've gone around the bend and bringing yourself back is incredibly hard to do and takes lots of practice. Remember the importance of modeling this behavior for your children. We all want our kids to learn to step away from being out of control and to rein themselves in. Having a lot of tools to use when you feel frustrated will help you "lose it" a lot less often. It will still happen though, so have a plan for that, too.

This is our chance to avoid being the parent we hate. If you feel awful when you yell, pick some other responses to use. If you insult your child or disdain him when it's his behavior you really don't like, you can change that. If you give up and give in when your child pushes back, you have options. People react badly (in a way they later regret) when they don't have a plan.

Why do soldiers train? Why do nurses and doctors practice life-saving techniques over and over again? Why do school children stand on windy sidewalks in line with their teachers during a fire drill? So that when a serious, emotionally charged situation arises, they don't have to think of a plan. Following a plan allows us to make decisions calmly beforehand and prevents us from simply reacting when we are frustrated, angry, or scared.

Let's talk about the nitty-gritty of what to do if (ha!) or when kids don't do as we've asked. Look at the list on the following page and pick some options that make sense to you. In the chapters that follow, I'll explain more about each and give some examples. Come up with a couple of specific examples of how you'll use them in your family. Talk them out with another adult (ideally your co-parent). Keep them in your pocket for the next time you feel the anger or frustration bubble up. I talk about all of these and more in the following chapters, but here are some highlights.

1. **Natural consequences (Chapter 55: "Let Life Teach the Lesson").** Behavior can change through nonintervention. Meaning, you don't rescue a child whose poor behavior has gotten her in trouble with someone else or has come to its own negative conclusion. You just wait until your child can listen to you and point out the life lesson she just experienced. This works well for younger children as well as older, as long as the consequences are not life-threatening.

2. **Remorse or regret (Chapter 55: "Let Life Teach the Lesson").** This involves relying on the good heart that beats inside every child (at least most of the time), and teaching empathy as a way of motivating behavior. Just like natural consequences, circumstances often lead a child to this outcome without our intervention. That leaves us with the challenge of letting a child feel bad for a while without stepping in to excuse his behavior. This is a great lesson, but it won't work every time. Sometimes kids (really all people) just don't care how others feel in that moment.

3. **Nonresponse (Chapter 56: "Nonresponse: I'm Not Ignoring You ...").** This is a great choice when you're working on manners, though it's also good for whining, talking back, and other rude behaviors. You simply continue on as if nothing had been said.

4. **Separation (Chapter 57: "Separation: We Now Interrupt Our Regularly Scheduled Programming ...").** For younger kids, this is a time-out. For siblings or friends, it may mean having to be in different spaces in your home. For older kids, it often means simply asking them to leave the room. Think of it as a change of venue to change an attitude or behavior.

5. **Reminding (Chapter 58: "Reminding: Did You Do That Yet?").** Your kids call this nagging, but it is an effective way of changing behavior when used sparingly.

6. **Losing privileges (Chapter 59: "Rights vs. Privileges")**. Aahhh, the mainstay of parenting tweens. When used well, this can be clear, predictable for parent and child, and really change behavior.

Some people are reading this and despairing. "She is so negative! Kids are good, you just have to show them more love to get great behavior." Kids *are* good. Often showing them more love does motivate great behavior. But kids are also walking egos and want what they want. Now. We need to have ways of shaping and motivating them to check their impulses, think before they speak or act, and consider others. Catching good behavior is often an excellent way of doing that, and for that I add:

7. **Gold star (Chapter 60: "Keep Your Focus Positive")**. Catch your child doing good. Have a plan for reinforcing good (or lack of bad) behaviors in a way that makes your child feel noticed and valued. Just keep in mind that the power of praise means too much can do damage as well.

8. **Turn the tables (Chapter 61: "Surprising Consequences")**. Take the behavior that is problematic and require the child to do the opposite. If a child is insulting, ask for three compliments or kind observations about the person she insulted. If an older sibling is blowing off a younger, make the older one responsible for helping the younger with some project they will both enjoy or find another team-building activity.

9. **Good gossip (Chapter 62: "Admire Your Kids")**. No matter whom you tell, kids love to know that you really do appreciate them. Describe your kid's most recent good deed to a neighbor, or a friend. Scan and e-mail a great teacher comment to a grandparent. Thank the heavens above for your child's efforts. Do these things out loud when your kiddo can hear you.

So pick some options that make sense to you and flip to those chapters for more specifics. Keep reading! A calmer future awaits you....

48

Say "No": You Won't Regret It

One day I was at a playground in another city while on vacation. My three-year-old climbed his way to the top of a pretty big slide, then stood up for a second on his way to sit down and slide. The slightly bigger girl behind him on the steps yelled "Go!" and pushed him down the slide. He came tumbling head over feet, and I ran to catch him. I grabbed him before he hit the ground and looked up at the little girl sitting triumphantly at the top of the slide with a big smile. "No!" I said. "Don't push people!"

I do know that this is a cardinal sin in today's society. We must never chastise another person's child, right? Especially from a family we don't know. But after years of parenting, camp counseling, and babysitting, it just popped out of my mouth. Sure enough, this little girl's mother came running over, looking very upset. She reached up for her daughter's hand, looked at me, and said something that shocked me to my core: "What are you doing? We never use that word!" I frantically searched my memory. Had I sworn at the little tyrant? I didn't *think* so, but was suddenly not 100 percent sure. After all, my pulse was only just coming back to normal after thinking my boy's brains might be smashed on the ground below the slide. "Um, what?" was my articulate reply.

"We don't say ..." her voice actually dropped to a whisper, " 'en – oh' to our daughter or anywhere near her, ever. It's terrible for children!" And then she gave my son a pitying glance—after all, we must say that horrible *word* to him—and hurried her daughter down the slide and away from my evil influence.

Please say no to your kids. As a matter of fact, "No" is a first line of parent defense. It is so useful and straightforward.

- Can I have that expensive and poorly made toy that I will only enjoy for five minutes? No.

- I want that treat even though I haven't washed what's left of the last one off my face. Nope.

- Can I sled off the roof? No. But thank you for asking.

- Mommy listen to me now! Not happening.

- Gimme that! No.

Why should we say no to our kids? Three important reasons:

1. It is what we mean. Clear communication, reasonable expectations, and consistency are what kids need to change their behavior. "No" is clear communication. It can be said with love.

2. Boundaries help kids. I can't say this enough. They need to know what is OK and what isn't. This word goes a long way toward making those limits clear.

3. They will hear it from others. Our kids need practice understanding what people mean when they say no, and how to respect it.

When I think of that family who never tells that little girl no, I imagine what she is going to be like when she is 13. Or 23. My biggest hope for that girl is that her parents realized "No" can be a loving thing to say to a child. And if they didn't? I can only hope one of my boys never brings her home to our house.

49

Hurting the One You Love

Has anyone with older kids ever looked at your young ones and told you, "Little kids, little problems. Big kids, big problems." When I was the mom of four boys under seven, that always felt a little like it missed the mark. After all, kids of all sizes can cause us big problems, right?

An older patient of mine told me a saying from her country: "Little kids? Headaches. Big kids? Heartaches." Often, parents of younger kids will project forward in their minds to raising teenagers. That can be a scary prospect. We transfer a lot of control to our kids by the time they are teens. Why do I mention this now?

Many years ago I heard a Father's Day lecture by a famous preacher. He said, "You'll win most of the battles with your teenagers while they are three, four, and five years old." I have seen this truth play out over and over again, in friends, patients, even my own family. We give young kids the structure they will depend on from the time they are born. They may still choose to battle us, but they will not be at all surprised when we give consequences, and stick to them.

Structured parenting, rules with clear expectations, and consequences to our kids' actions. These can't prevent the heartaches of the teen years, but they will build a foundation on which our kids can rely.

I hate it when my children get in trouble. Selfishly, it almost always means that I will have a worse day. No TV for you? You're going to be hanging around the kitchen while your brothers are watching a movie, actively frustrated and miserable. I like you too much to enjoy your suffering, and now I don't get any quiet time either.

Over and over again parents tell me they want their kids to behave well, but, "I can't stand to punish them." Parents speak to me of empathy for their kids' suffering, "I hated being in trouble as a child." Moms, especially, speak of guilt, "I feel so bad if I deny her something she really wants." Most parents feel the backlash of a child's anger, "If I take away something as a consequence, he hates me for days!"

Yup. That is all true, and it's all hard. But you know what? It doesn't matter.

Your kids can count on you. You will do what is right, even when it's hard because you love your kids that much.

Some years ago, one of our boys was having trouble learning to respect other peoples' bodies as private. He got in trouble several times for not respecting those boundaries. Things seemed to be going well for a few months, and then I got a call from the principal. This child was in his office because he'd been drumming on the bottom of another child in school, and without her permission.

That afternoon, we were supposed to go to a big carnival that is only in our town once a year. We go every year, and the boys and I really look forward to it. When my son got off the bus, his first words were, "Do I still get to go to the carnival?" Nope. I'd gotten a sitter so that he would stay home while I took his brothers. My son cried. His brothers cried. I cried, too. When he saw that he was totally flabbergasted. "If it makes *you* sad, just say I can go!"

I explained to him that I couldn't let him go. "I am hugely disappointed that we can't go to the carnival together. But it's much more important that we raise you to be a man who knows how to respect peoples' bodies and privacy, than that I get to go with you to this carnival." My disappointment and determination seemed to make more of an impression on my kids than the punishment itself. We agreed that he needed to write a letter of apology to this girl, and one to her parents as well. If he got those done, then he could play a board game with the babysitter while he waited for us to come home. He did it, but he was clearly angry for the rest of the night.

The next morning my son woke up in a surprisingly decent mood. He had two things to say to me. "You take this parenting thing really seriously." And "364 more days until I can go to the carnival!"

ASK DOCTOR G

Parent Q: Is spanking ever OK?

I am opposed to corporal punishment. On this topic I agree completely with the American Academy of Pediatrics: Spanking does not change behavior for the better and can be very damaging. Causing kids physical pain to improve their behavior has never been shown to work.

Some cultures use pain, such as smacking, beating, spanking, cuffing, pinching, yanking, and so many more methods, to correct children.

When I speak in communities where this is common, I always ask the adults, "Were you beat as a child?" When the answer is yes, I have one follow-up question, "Did it work to make you behave better?" The answer has always been "No." These adults tell me that they became better at avoiding adults, hiding from them, and resenting them, but did not in any way change the behavior that had gotten them in trouble in the first place.

We have to be willing to cause our kids emotional pain. We have to be willing to manage our disappointment, our empathy, our guilt. Nobody ever changed a behavior without some discomfort.

You don't need more friends.

If your child always likes you, I'm going to go out on a limb and guess that you are making things a little too easy for her. It's been said many times by many parents: "I'm not here to be your friend." Be the parent. It's much harder, but a lot more important.

When you lose motivation, remember your goal. You want to raise a child into an adult you can respect and admire. To do that, you'll have to cause some pain. You'll have to get her out of that comfortable spot where rules are to be negotiated. Instead of being a friend, you're giving her the skills she needs to be a good person. You're doing the right thing!

50

Do One Thing and Do It Well

Every year, on January 2, patients come to see me who tell me a story like this: "Doc, I quit smoking yesterday and I'm going to the gym every day and I'm gonna stop eating all junk food and take that vitamin sitting on my counter every morning. And I quit caffeine." Every year, for each of these patients, these "resolutions" last about three days.

Why do they crash and burn? Three reasons:

1. **There is no plan.** The Nike version of change—Just Do It—works a lot better when you're getting a 3 million dollar sponsorship check for your efforts.

2. **The focus is on the negative.** We really don't ask each other, "What aren't you going to do today?" We are wired to think about action, not avoidance. Thinking about what we can't or won't do makes most people feel frustrated and resentful.

3. **Too many changes at once.** Whatever behaviors are bothering you at your house, whatever resolutions you may have for your family, don't fall into these traps.

Engage your parenting partner.

Question: If you implement a behavior change, what does your partner do?

   A. Jump on the bandwagon.

   B. Stay out of it.

   C. Make fun of the new plan, and you, in front of the kids.

I'm hoping the answer is A. If the answer is B, that's alright, too. If the answer is C? A little marriage counseling might make sense before parenting changes....

If you are single parenting, this is one time that life will be easier. If you are not single parenting, you'll see more success if you're able to get your partner to buy into this process. Change is hard, but it's much, much harder if you have to struggle against the other adult at home even while you're reshaping your child's expectations and behavior.

ASK∘DOCTOR G

Parent Q: I heard you speak and I really want to make some changes at my house. My husband is not on board. How can I get him to believe?

*T*he best way to get him to agree to put forth the effort is to figure out what goal you share. What hopes do you and your partner share for your child? Do you both want to raise someone who speaks respectfully? Are you aligned in your desire to raise a child who can handle it when life doesn't go her way, and recover? Are both of you tired of the arguing? Perhaps you've both talked about wanting a child who knows how to grow up and get a job.

Focus on the goal you both share most strongly. Now you just need to pick a behavior that is clearly linked to that goal. If your partner can agree that the goal is valid and the behavior change would be great, you're much more likely to get the support you need in following up on consequences. If your partner is really skeptical, focus on the goal he or she has for your child or your home, something you know bothers him or her.

Pick one thing.

What one change would most impact your home in a great way? Would you like to end the bickering or tattling or whining? Do you want each child to do one chore that benefits the whole family? Is homework the time that makes you not want to be in your house? Maybe talking back is the thorn in your side. Whatever it is, pick the thing you (and your partner) agree would be the most valuable to change.

If you're feeling very uncertain, pick what feels to you to be the easiest thing to change. Perhaps your kids only complain a little, but you'd like to get rid of it. Maybe they are helping out but need a few reminders and you'd like them to step up without any nagging. Picking a fairly straightforward task can give your whole family the confidence to move on to something bigger.

Once you've changed one thing successfully, you will have lots more motivation to go on to the next item on your list. Very similar to dieting, small successes often empower us to be persistent and see the greater change we desire.

Do a reality check.

Are you aiming for a behavior that (a) your child could actually do, and (b) that your family can sustain? Kids come with a blueprint. You cannot change a shy child into an outgoing one because you decide to try. Similarly, you cannot train a child to have an organized, spotless room every day in a house full of messiness in all the other rooms.

Wendy Mogel, in a fantastic book called *The Blessing of a Skinned Knee* says, "Grow the tree you've got." If you moved into a home with an evergreen by the front door, but you had always dreamed of having a Japanese Maple, you might resent that evergreen. But even if you water and prune and fertilize it, following the directions for a maple, it will always be an evergreen. And you could miss the joy of a beautiful evergreen. If you got an artistic, dramatic, highly empathic child, but had always pictured raising an athletic, easy-going, quiet kid, you could spend your time trying to train your child to be something he fundamentally isn't. You have the power to make yourself miserable and miss the joy. Don't do it. Help your child to live her own nature while doing and being good at it. This, by the way, does NOT mean a rude child has to be rude. Manners *can* be changed.

If you're not certain about your reality check, ask someone else who knows and loves your child, someone you trust, for his or her opinion.

Do that one thing well.

Now that you've chosen one thing, and your partner agrees, it's time to get specific. Let's take whining as an example.

You're going to outlaw whining at your house. Make a list—and write it down.

- **Who.** Everyone. This means Mom and Dad don't get to whine, either.

- **What.** That whiny tone of voice must end.

- **When.** As soon as you've explained the plan to the whole family.

- **Where.** Wherever either parent is with any kiddo in the family. Don't try to enforce this rule when you are not around.

- **Why.** Whining does not make people want to help you. When we let you whine, we are setting you up for pain and suffering once you get out into the real world.

- **How.** Decide with your partner on the consequences for whining. The easiest is to say that you are not going to say yes to a request that is whined. Ever. It will be as if the child didn't say anything at all.

Focus on the positive.

Just like my patients who are discouraged by three days of everything they can't do, our kids get easily frustrated by hearing what they are not allowed to do. As silly as it might sound, framing this in the positive can make a difference, especially for kids under 10.

"From now on, we're going to teach you how to ask for things in ways that work."

Come up with a list of words that replace whining. Here are some words you might like to associate with your child's needs:

- Polite

- Positive

- Respectful

• Assertive

• Creative

Really, follow whatever makes sense for you and your child in your family. This list of great attributes will help you remember why you're bothering with this behavior change in the first place!

So now you have a plan: A positive plan, with your partner's agreement, to make one change.

51

The Family Meeting

In my husband's family, all important conversations occurred at the kitchen table. From choosing a college to talking about who may or may not have crashed the family car, their tradition was to settle in around the table as a group and figure it out. The kids might or might not like the outcome of some of those conversations, but it was a place where everyone knew his or her opinion mattered and would be heard.

Years ago, a dean at the medical school where I trained spoke to a large group of students. "The most important meeting of my week," he intoned, "occurs every Sunday evening in my living room. Attending are myself, my wife, and our children." He explained that this was the meeting of schedules, of needs, of minds, that guided what everyone would do that week: how obligations would get met, how questions would be answered, how fun would be found. I always imagined doing exactly the same thing once I had a family of my own.

It turns out, I'm not that organized. Our "family meetings" happen in the kitchen, or on somebody's bed, or in the car. With a family of six, and parents who work opposite schedules, any time we find ourselves all awake and in the same place is cause for both celebration and scheduling.

Family meetings are excellent glue. They stick us together, and they help us stick to the goals we have for our kids and as a family. The meetings can build loyalty among us as a group, and teach our kids respect and responsibility. Not to mention some resilience, as (at least in our home) these are rarely quiet, simple gatherings. These are often loud, take a fair amount of redirection, and get off on a tangent almost every time. But we drag them back on course and get to the point (eventually).

Why am I inserting this chapter about the family meeting in the "How To" section of getting behaviors to change? Because it's just about time for one. Even if you've never before had a family meeting. And really, of course you have; you just may not have called it that. Think about what you've accomplished so far:

1. You decided to make a change.

2. You picked a behavior.

3. You (and your partner) decided on a plan.

Nothing is going to change, though, until you let the rest of the family (those who live in your home) in on the project. Calling a family meeting might sound too formal for your family, but that could also be to your benefit. You're making a change, and you want your whole family to take that seriously. Starting a new tradition will get their attention.

If you, or any of your kids, are visual learners, bring a few school supplies to your meeting. A poster, or a whiteboard, a piece of paper, and some markers should do it.

Get everyone together and explain what a family meeting is:

• A time to sit together, with phones and headphones elsewhere.

• To talk about one or more topics that affect the whole family.

• Everyone gets to express his or her opinion respectfully.

• To leave with a plan.

Explain what a family meeting isn't: a democracy. The parents are still in charge. You will decide on the plan after hearing everyone's opinion. Those opinions might change the plan and might not.

Now get to the point. Let's use the whining example. "We've decided that we need a house with no whining. And we need a plan."

• Explain (briefly) your reasons. You are actually doing this to make your home more peaceful and your own life easier, but also so that your kids will be easier for other people to like and more likely to get what they need from adults.

- Make sure they know what you mean by "whining." Prepare yourself for 10 minutes of "examples."

- Outline the plan: "If you whine, you get one reminder. But you will not get what you're asking for until you can ask politely and without whining."

- Now get your kids involved.

  - What should the consequences be if we remind someone and that person whines again?

  - What should the reward be once our whole family goes a week without whining?

- Write it down.

- Ask for questions: "What if I'm sick? Or hurt? Or he's annoying me?" No whining. At all, to anyone.

- Plan a follow-up meeting to check in on how it's going, and see if the reward has been earned.

  And now for the hard part ... sticking to the plan.

52

Consistency: Planting the Flag

"Do you have a flag?" Any Eddie Izzard fans out there? No? Well, in this comedy sketch, the British land in India, where they raise the Union Jack and proclaim: "We claim this land in the name of Her Majesty The Queen." The native Indians say, "But we already live here!" The British soldiers look momentarily flustered and then ask, "Do you have a flag?" When the Indians admit that they do not, the British regain their confidence and once more claim the land.

This is an excellent guide to parenting young kids. You need to plant your flag.

Let me explain what I mean. Once you draw a boundary around your child's behavior, such as "no more whining," that line can't change. Our kids need to know what is acceptable and what is not. Good communication of clear expectations gives kids a solid foundation on which to stand.

Boundaries help kids. They teach respect, responsibility, and resilience. Society has boundaries; we call them laws. Schools have rules. Our kids need to learn the skills that will allow them to understand boundaries and live within them. I don't want my kids to obey every rule for the rest of their lives, but they have to know how to follow rules in order to learn which ones to break, and when.

Have you ever spent time in a kindergarten classroom? The rules are written and posted on the walls. The children learn the rules, and can recite them whenever the teacher asks. The kids themselves remind each other of the rules and enforce them by letting the teacher know if someone breaks one. The kids are confident about what is expected of them, and constantly reassured by the structure. Kindergarten teachers are masters of consistency.

A rule is a promise. I tell my child, "Hitting is never OK. If you hit someone you will have to go sit by yourself, apologize, and then find a way to make it better." I am making a promise that hitting is actually never OK. I promise that there will be a consequence every time he hits someone. I promise that I will raise him to be someone who does not hit in anger.

When I enforce those consequences, I'm proving to my sons that they can trust me. If they are hit or are hitting, I will teach this lesson. Every time. If I let it go even once, I make them all (not just the kiddo who hit) more likely to hit. Even worse, I am breaking that promise and making them question whether or not they can believe me. Can kids forgive that on occasion? Absolutely. It has to be rare, though.

So you've picked a behavior. You've talked to your partner, and decided on a plan. You've had your family meeting and announced the new boundary. Now you have to stick to it. Consistency. I won't lie, it's really hard!

A few things to think about when planting that flag in the ground:

- **Don't plant a flag you can't defend.** I have made the mistake of saying to my child, "If you do that again we're going home ..." and then suddenly realized that we couldn't leave. I was hosting the baby shower where we were. Have you ever said, "That's it. No TV for a month!" and then thought, "Oh no, what did I just do?"

- **Take the do-over.** Kids are very open to the idea of a "re-do." This is a concept they use in their own games all the time. So if you promise a consequence and then realize immediately that you can't enforce it, call a "do over." Communicate clearly and say "Wait, do over. We can't actually leave right now. But, if you do that again you will sit on that bottom step until this baby shower is over." Umm, yes, I have had that exact conversation. How did you know?

- **Don't plant a flag you won't defend.** Kids, especially young kids, do not understand a rule that exists for a few weeks and then gets forgotten. So pick something that is really important, with lots of motivation for you to see it through.

- **Not every situation needs a flag.**

  - Sometimes we can just explain to a child what is going on and how we need her to behave in that moment. No promise or threat is necessary. "The way you spoke to my friend was not respectful. Please go apologize."

  - Certain behaviors do not deserve a warning. Kids four years old and older know that some behaviors are never OK. If a child picks up a fragile item and smashes it on the floor out of anger (or to see what happens), it is really a good idea to say, "And now we're leaving." Do not get caught up in thinking that you should have a debate with your child about expectations in that moment. Just apologize, sweep up if you need to, and leave.

- **Try not to plant a flag and then desert the field.** Every once in a while, I will give a child a consequence and then realize that I'll be out of town for a big part of that punishment, or leaving him with a babysitter. It can be a burden to give someone else the responsibility for holding a child to a consequence that wasn't his or her idea. Negotiate this one beforehand. If you think it will be hard on your spouse or in-law or babysitter to enforce, just change the timing. Kids six and older will be able to understand, "You're on screen time restriction next week because of this choice you made." If you do stick someone else with the job of enforcing a consequence, think seriously about coming home with gifts. For the adult.

Consistency is *the* hardest part of being a parent. Once we've set a boundary, we need to enforce it 99.9 percent of the time. I'm so often tempted to give my kids a "break." He's tired. He's hungry. He's sick. He's upset. I can think of more excuses for my kids' bad behavior than *they* can. Also, I'm lazy. It would often be a lot easier to just drop it. I don't enjoy arguing with my kids about their behavior, and I don't enjoy their misery or anger when there is a consequence to endure.

Do it anyway.

It has to be so rare when you bend a rule that your children stop and ask why. This should be shocking behavior on your part, a real departure from usual. If it is that surprising, then you will be able to use the change to teach your kids that you are showing some compassion and flexibility. Mostly this is because changing the boundary is almost never the best thing to do.

Your children will learn faster and adapt better if you stick to your plan. They will trust you and respect you more. Your kids will be stronger and you will get the behavior you want without being the parent you hate.

53

It's Still a Gift if You Ask for It

In the weeks before your birthday, have you ever thought to yourself, "I wish someone would get me...." Imagine you ask your spouse or mom or friend for exactly what you want, "You know, Target is selling a miniature ceramic pug dog painted purple with fake emerald eyes that I just love!" When your birthday comes and you open the purple pug, is it still a gift? Yes. You told someone who loves you exactly what would make you happy. You gave him or her a gift, too. You took out all the guesswork, all the uncertainty and searching and nervousness that it wouldn't be right.

Do that for your children. Figure out exactly what you would like your child to say when you ask or tell them to do something. Then tell them.

First, let me give credit where it's due. Ever heard the truism that alcoholics often comfort themselves by hanging out with someone who drinks even more? The theory is that the people around them normalize the behavior. Well, I have four kids. No, this is not when I confess that you have to drink to have this many children. However, I do have several friends with more kids than me. And on occasion I have been known to think to myself, "See? This is totally normal!" In truth, it is from one of these moms (and she's not crazy at all, most of the time) that I learned this important lesson.

I was simply sick of the whining and the attitude I got whenever I asked my boys to do something they didn't feel like doing. It didn't seem respectful to me to hear "Whhhhhhhyyyyyy?" when asked to move something, go to the bathroom, put on shoes, or help in any way. And did I mention it's annoying? So I called this mom of more-and-older-kids and (OK I admit it) whined. "Do you have any idea how to get my kids to stop talking back when I tell them to do something?" "Sure," she said. "Tell them what to say instead. Say it for them until they get it." So I picked, "Yes, Mom." If a child is acting especially snarky I change it to "Yes, ma'am."

What does that look like? It's time to leave the house for school. Breakfast is (sort of) eaten. "Go put your shoes on please." Your tired, just-not-a-morning-person first-grader says, "I want to plaaaayyy." Look at your child and say in your most pleasant, genuine tone of voice, "Yes, Mom." When she looks at you as if you have suddenly grown a second head, move closer to her, look in her eyes, smile, and say (in exactly the tone you want her to use), "Yes, Mom." If she is still not catching on, explain that she should say this and go put on her shoes, and *then* you'll be happy to answer any questions she has or explain your reasons. If she gets up to go put on the shoes and skips the verbal response, stop her gently or move in front of her, make eye contact, and say, "Yes, Mom." You can make this playful and fun. You can be stern. Use a goofy animal voice or use your most serious I-mean-it-or-you're-in-trouble eyes. But be firm. Don't let her move past this task and don't talk about anything else until you hear the phrase you want.

The lesson to your children here is twofold. Doing what he's been told or asked to do matters. Responding respectfully to the person who has spoken to him matters as well. This response on his part fulfills several goals at once. Responding when spoken to is polite. This will help him in school, work, relationships, and at home. Speaking respectfully to his parent even if he doesn't like what he's being told to do will make him more likely to do what's been asked (it's no guarantee) and it will make his argument easier for you to hear.

Tone of voice matters. After you have been at this for a while, your child may use your response phrase to imply lots of other things. Maybe my kids are especially gifted at this (doesn't every parent think his or her child is gifted in some way?). She can use the words "Yes, Mom," but make them sound exactly like "This is so dumb" or "You're so mean" or "I'm the most oppressed child in the history of the universe." Really, it's an art form. Don't ignore this. Your phrase needs the words *and* the tone of voice that makes it respectful. Again, you don't have to get into a debate or an argument about this. Simply look in your child's eyes and use the tone you're looking for her to use when saying "Yes, Mom" until you hear it back the way you want it. Ignore every request, argument, and entreaty until you hear what you need. You can offer hints

ASK∘DOCTOR G

Parent Q: My four-year-old son just naturally talks in a whiny voice. It's like nails on a chalkboard. He just doesn't know how to speak any differently. How can I teach him?

W*hen* your beautiful child whines a request, just repeat it back with the words and tone you want. Children learn to speak by repeating what they hear. They can learn to speak nicely in the same way. Specifically for whining, if you keep repeating it back and forth but your child can't remove all the whine from his words, tell him to whisper. It is nearly impossible to whine and whisper at the same time.

like, "I'm not actually answering you because I'm still waiting for 'Yes, Mom' and to see the shoes on your feet."

Many parents complain bitterly about being ignored by their kids. Many young people are experts at using silence aggressively. Make sure your child knows that, in your family, every respectful question or statement gets an answer, even from siblings. Ignoring is hurtful and home is no place for it. Later we are going to talk about using ignoring to modify behavior. We will talk about how to make it clear that you are ignoring a behavior and not a person when you do that. Keep in mind that interrupting is not a respectful question or statement and may sometimes be ignored. With that in mind, make sure you are not ignoring your children or partner just because you don't feel like answering.

This is (and I know this word makes some people uncomfortable) teaching your child to obey. Obey: "To comply with or follow instructions, commands, wishes or instructions," according to the dictionary. You have the right to expect this of your child. Don't get freaked out that I'm encouraging parents to be mean and dictatorial with no thought for their child's humanity. Your kids have rights, too; we'll get to that later. I stand by this though: You have the obligation to teach your child how to obey.

Consider an emergency situation. You awake one night to find there is a fire in your home. There simply is no time for debate, conversation, or explanation. Your child must know how to obey. Some parents believe that they do not need to teach this skill to their kids, that in the event of an emergency their child's common sense will tell them it isn't time to argue. This has *not* been my experience. If you are still skeptical, imagine a more common situation. You and your children are walking down the street and you see someone walking toward you that you think may be dangerous. When you unexpectedly tell your children to enter a store with you or gather close to you, you must be met by your "Yes, Mom." Teach this potentially life-saving skill and make it second nature.

54

Lying Is a Separate Problem

Of all the things our kids do that frustrate us as parents, lying is a crucial challenge to address. Lying makes us feel hurt, betrayed, angry, and sometimes helpless. One of the most common questions I get from parents is: "How can I get my child to stop lying?!"

Why do kids lie?

Kids lie, in general, because it seems like a good solution to a problem. In an effort not to disappoint someone he loves, to not get in trouble, or to not be held accountable for an action, a child latches on to lying as the easiest answer. Kids lie even when they're not in trouble for various reasons: to be more interesting, to control a situation, to get sympathy or attention, to see what happens, or because the truth is—for whatever reason—not acceptable. Lying is not the same at every age.

- **Toddlers.** Kids this young genuinely don't know the difference between truth and make believe. Everything is equally possible, and "tell the truth" has no more meaning than "tell a story." It takes some more cognitive development to get this complex idea.

- **Preschoolers.** As children transition into the reasoning and knowledge they'll need, they still hang onto certain beliefs. One of those beliefs is that saying something makes it true. Repeating that "fact" a few times makes it indisputable. So when a child keeps saying, "I didn't hit her!" she is becoming more and more convinced. After a few repetitions, she could easily pass a lie detector test.

- **Ages 5 – 7.** Most early elementary schoolers are learning the difference between fact and fiction. As a matter of fact, this is a common exercise in language arts, so you can thank your child's teacher for help with this issue. Kids this age will make up stories and present them as true in order to change a person's thinking or get a desired result. They don't like the truth so they try something made up and see what happens.

- **Ages 8 – 10.** Most lies at this age are to avoid getting in trouble. In school and at home, kids are learning what adults will check on and what they might be able to fib about. The child is hoping to avoid a punishment, or disappointing someone whose opinion matters.

- **Ages 11 – 12.** As middle schoolers bond tightly to friends, they will often use lies to prove their loyalty to their peers and their willingness to let family ties loosen. This is developmentally normal, but not OK for us to allow. They need to learn how to bond with friends without sacrificing family.

Why is it damaging?

Lies are a normal part of childhood. Like hitting, tantrums, attitude, and bullying, lying is something almost every child tries. Our job is to convince him that the behavior is not worth the cost.

Lies wound parents, kids, and relationships.

When a child lies, it undermines our faith in our parenting. As parents, we constantly look for "proof" that we are doing a good job with our kids. Lying feels like exactly the opposite; it's proof that our child is not a good person and we are doing a bad job of leading her. That is not true, but the behavior is hurtful.

Kids who lie lose self-esteem.

Dishonesty teaches kids that what they did, who they are, and what they saw wasn't good enough, and more, the only way to be good enough is to lie. Bit by bit, deceiving others—especially those you love—makes a child feel like a terrible person. This can drive even young kids toward other unhealthy behaviors, as well as true sadness and dissatisfaction with life.

Kids who lie hurt their reputation.

At school, with family, with coaches, with mentors, and also with friends, we all look differently at someone who will say what's easy instead of what's true. As parents, it is our responsibility to see this bigger picture, even if our kids are not able to understand the repercussions of their actions.

Lies weaken relationships.

Talking to each other is a fundamental part of love and family. The realization that any conversation could be false or misleading makes people isolated from each other. Family members often shut down or distance themselves from someone who can't be relied on to tell the truth.

How can we stop it?

1. **Explain why it matters.** In a long series of conversations that start when kids are very young, help your family understand why you value honesty and just how important that value is to you. Use books, stories, TV, and movies to discuss lying with children. Ask their opinion, and discuss their experiences and feelings.

2. **Practice telling truth from lie.** When a child is **not** in the hot seat, talk about stories and help her realize what is true and what is made up. Praise creativity while helping her understand that creativity is not OK when reporting on an event that actually happened.

   a. **Toddlers and preschoolers** can listen to a story and then try telling the facts of what actually happened.

   b. **Elementary school–aged kids** benefit from talking about why kids lie and what they could do instead.

c. **Middle schoolers** will be able to explain exaggeration and metaphor, and how they can be used to make a point but are not actually facts.

3. **Separate the lie from everything else.** If your child does something wrong and then lies about it, separate out the consequences. Our seven-year-old broke a window with a soccer ball while at a friend's house. For breaking the window, he needed to apologize to the owner of the home and save up money to help pay for the new window. For lying about it, however, there was a much harder consequence. He was not allowed to go to friends' houses for a long time. This was to make the point that we value trust above all. We had to know he would tell the truth if something went wrong.

4. **Condemn behavior, not children.** The important lesson here for children is that they will make mistakes, but we can be trusted to love them anyway. There is no need to lie about a mistake or bad choice because, with honesty, we will correct the behavior while still respecting the child. Also, kids believe what we say about them. If you call a child a liar, then that is what he will be.

5. **Point out all the times that truth benefits your family.** Kids understand trust when they see it in action.

a. **Toddlers and preschoolers** love it when we cuddle a sad mood away or comfort a hurt. Point out that this is trust—knowing that a child is bringing a real concern and genuinely needs our time and attention. They can trust us to give them the love that will help them feel better.

b. **Kids aged 5–10** need to be able to tell us their side of the story when something goes wrong. As we help them problem solve, we are demonstrating our trust in their explanation. Mention how much you value that, especially when a child is willing to put herself in a bad light in order to give you the whole truth.

c. **In middle school** tweens will often latch onto an accusation of lying and try to turn it into a debate about trust or privacy. Explain to kids this age that trust is earned and can be broken.

Once it's broken it is very difficult and time-consuming to repair. Remind your children of all the times they count on us to trust them and help them see that breaking it is not worth getting out of a penalty.

6. **Don't lie.** This, I think, is hardest for us as parents. We can't lie to our kids. For younger children, lies are hurtful and confusing. For older children, our lies become their excuse for their own, and are no less painful. I know this presents quandaries for parents, so here are a few suggestions:

   a. **If you don't know, say so.** This is great modeling for kids—knowing everything is not a reasonable goal, but saying you don't know and will work to find out is admirable.

   b. **If you don't want to answer something** it is OK to say "That is not your business" or "I'm not ready to discuss this with you." Kids may not like these answers, but you remain trustworthy.

   c. **Consider telling the truth about the tooth fairy.** Imaginary creatures are wonderful experiences for kids, but when your child corners you to find out the truth, consider asking, "Do you really want to know?" If this child is after the truth, seriously consider giving it to him. It is more important that he knows he can trust you than that he has one more year with the Easter Bunny. If you do give him the real story, then let him know you are trusting him to keep it private between the two of you and not talk to any other kids about it.

Trust is what we are building and preserving by teaching kids not to lie. As one of my sons explained to me when he was eight, "Parents don't know half the trouble they start when they lie to kids or let us lie to them."

55

Let Life Teach the Lesson

Do you hate punishing your kids? Most of us do! I ask huge groups of parents, "Why do you hesitate to give your kids a consequence when they behave badly?" See if any of these answers ring true for you:

- I don't have the time/energy.

- They get so angry at me!

- It's hard to think of a good one.

- I don't want them to feel bad.

- I forget to enforce it.

- It doesn't actually work.

Some of the chapters in this section give ideas for behavior management that solve these problems. But the best way to avoid having to think up a consequence that you have the energy for, can remember, actually works, and takes the focus off of you (and onto the behavior) is to let life teach the lesson for you.

This means one of our biggest jobs as a parent is to get out of the way when our kids' actions have natural consequences. Before I talk about why, here are a few examples so you can see what I mean.

- **Toddlers.** Your precious two-year-old has a friend over. That friend grabs a beloved truck from your child's hands to play with it. Your child grabs the truck back and bashes the friend over the head with it! You comfort the hurt child and chastise your own. The best learning happens when he wants that child to come back over and the kiddo doesn't want to. Instead of begging that mom to change the best friend's mind, just show empathy for your child's sadness, but also help him make the connection. "I understand why you're sad. What do you think might help him forgive you for hitting him on the head?" When your child draws a picture or card to bring to the friend (for example), you're not punishing him—you're just letting a life experience teach him a lesson.

- **Preschoolers.** Your four-year-old will not leave her older sister alone. She loves big sis so much she wants to be in her space, her face, and her stuff. She goes too far and takes (and ruins) some makeup, and your older daughter bans her from her bedroom. Don't intervene. When we break a rule it has relationship consequences. If your younger daughter comes to you complaining, ask what she thinks might rebuild her older sister's trust? What could help repair the relationship?

- **Ages 5–7.** Your child wants to bring his favorite toy to the zoo. You are worried that it will get lost. You explain clearly to your child that bringing the action figure is a big risk, and if it gets lost he may never see it again. If he brings the toy and loses it, you don't have to do any "I told you so." Just don't buy another one to replace it.

- **Ages 8–10.** Your child stays up hours late under her covers reading a book. Parents have contacted me several times to ask, "How can I possibly punish a child for loving to read?" I totally sympathize and can tell you from very personal experience that you can just do what (ahem) my parents did. No "consequence" except exhaustion the next day, and no excuses for getting up late or missing obligations.

- **Ages 11–12.** You get a call from school: "Mom! I forgot my (science fair project, band instrument, gym uniform, homework)." Whatever it is feels to your child like an emergency. You know it's an opportunity. An opportunity to stop nagging and let him learn for himself the importance of putting the work in his backpack, or getting up five minutes earlier, or making a list. Don't drive that missing item to school! Whatever consequences happen at school are well-deserved. Show empathy but stand strong.

When life teaches the lesson for our kids, we can just go along for the ride. The problem we face as parents is to restrain our own urges to rescue our kids. We want to fix the hurt, solve the problem, be the hero. Don't do it. Don't miss the chance for your child to learn and grow.

Remorse and regret.

When our kids feel bad, we feel bad. That empathy is normal, and healthy ... to a point. However, don't let it stand in the way of being a great parent. Don't let your empathy or guilt control your choices. Kids need to feel the consequences of their actions, and often the consequence of a poor choice is remorse or regret.

Remorse means feeling sorry you did something. Regret is wishing you hadn't done it. These are powerful motivators for kids as they work to make a different choice the next time. So, if a situation leads to remorse or regret in a child, stifle your urge to excuse them, or make them feel better before it's time.

- **Toddlers.** Your toddler bites or hits you, and you're hurt. Let her know it hurt, and that it will take a while to feel better. Don't say, "It's OK, I'm alright!" It isn't, and you aren't.

- **Preschoolers.** Your child breaks the TV remote, which he wasn't supposed to touch. Your husband is angry that the remote is broken and storms out of the room. Your son feels bad; that is normal and healthy. Encourage him to find a way to make his dad feel better.

- **Ages 5–7.** At family dinner, your seven-year-old asked Grandma why she's fat. Grandma was very hurt and went home upset. Your daughter needs to understand that her words led to that reaction, so that she can adequately apologize and hold her tongue next time.

- **Ages 8–10.** The nine-year-old twins were wrestling for fun, but one got genuinely angry, picked up a toy, and bashed his brother with it. On the trip to the hospital for stitches, the aggressor feels terrible. That's fair, right?

- **Ages 11 – 12.** Your daughter told her best friend's secret to someone else. That friend is furious and doesn't want to come for the sleepover they had planned. Don't intervene. Your daughter should not have told that secret, and her remorse is helping her learn an important lesson.

There is a big difference between letting a child feel guilty and making a child feel guilty. Using remorse to help a child regret an action is a good lesson. In that case, don't go out of your way to make the child feel better by excusing his behavior. That teaches the child to look for excuses, rather than holding himself accountable. On the other hand, don't go out of your way looking for ways to make a child feel guilt; this is not an effective behavior change strategy, and can trample a child's self-esteem.

What about those times when there is no natural consequence? Or the natural consequence alone isn't working? For kids to change a behavior, they have to see the connection between the behavior and what happens next. Use that anytime you can to reinforce what you need your child to learn.

- **Toddlers.** Your little one needs to get in the car but wants to keep looking at the book in her hands. If she can get in the car without fussing, she can bring the book along. If she pitches a fit, or hurls the book across the room, the book stays home while you put her in the car.

- **Preschoolers.** Your child gets down from the table with food left on his plate. "I'm done!" You are certain that his hunger is not satisfied and that he should eat more. "I'd like you to have some more dinner. This is your last chance for dinner, no snacks tonight." If he decides to put his plate away, all you need to do is not give a snack later when he is hungry. He won't starve and he will (start to) learn!

- **Ages 5 – 7.** The six-year-old yells, "I hate you, Dad!" And just like that, the planned trip to the amusement park is off for that child. Why? "I don't spend fun time with people who are disrespectful to me. I hope you won't either."

- **Ages 8 – 10.** Your fourth-grader has a friend over and they come up with a "game" of scaring your kindergartner. Your younger child is crying, you intervene, and the older boys apologize. After the friend leaves, you explain that your son will not be allowed any more playdates for the week, and needs to spend some time with his younger brother playing and showing kindness.

- **Ages 11–12.** Your seventh-grader has Instagram on her phone. A friend shares a nasty picture of someone else they know and your daughter comments and reshares the picture. Most kids have trouble passing up the opportunity to join in this kind of social media communication but you are not about to let any kind of bullying continue. That phone is once again yours. It doesn't teach the whole lesson—there are conversations to have here, and apologies to be made—but she has certainly proved that she is not mature enough to have a phone for the next while.

Coming up with consequences that "fit the crime" can take some creativity. Your child may have some good ideas about her own consequences. It's amazing how stern kids are with themselves sometimes. I also highly recommend crowd-sourcing. Talk to a trusted friend or family member with older kids and ask what he suggests—not only to make your child feel the sting but to help drive home the lesson.

The point to consequences is not suffering, it's growth. Change is hard and learning doesn't happen all at once. Whenever you can, just get out of the way and let school, friends, siblings, and life itself teach the lesson your child needs most to learn in that moment.

56

Nonresponse: I'm Not Ignoring You ...

... I'm just not answering you. My husband says the thing he misses the most about his life BK (Before Kids) is finishing a conversation, or even a sentence, uninterrupted. It can wreck your train of thought and is pretty annoying for the person you are talking to as well. Interrupting is the best across-the-ages example of a time to use nonresponse to change behavior.

Before we talk about nonresponse, I want to differentiate this from ignoring. Why shouldn't you occasionally ignore your kids? Simple. Do you want your teenagers to ignore you? They will try for sure. If you have been ignoring them intermittently since they were small, though, you will have a much harder time making the case that this is rude, unacceptable behavior, right? To ignore means (among other things) to reject an overture. This is not the same as noticing an attempt at communication, and then choosing not to respond because it's not a polite attempt.

I'm in the office seeing a family of six. Who in the world would be crazy enough to have four kids, let alone bring them all to the doctor for appointments on the same day? Well, I would for one, and so would these parents. The kids are all there for well-child checks and (gulp) shots and are a little wired up with boredom and nerves about going to the doctor. They are bouncing around the room, playing with the equipment, diving into the red biohazard trash, and trying to spin on the stool I'm sitting on (all kids do this, not just yours). The parents are talking over and around the chaos, pulling children off of each other without really breaking stride in their conversation with me. This is different; usually parents are very flustered during this part of the visit and I need to just be patient while they stop a hundred or so times to talk to their kids and answer all the kids' interruptions.

Eventually I notice that these parents are not answering their kids when they interrupt. Instead, the parent will continue talking to me, stopping just for a quick second to do something unusual. I want you to try to picture this. The dad who is being interrupted will close his lips, put a forefinger against his chin, and look quizzically at the child speaking, and then go right back to talking to me. Every time, the interrupting child stopped talking and waited. The parent then touched that child in some nice way for a second. At the end of the visit, I asked the parents: How are you getting your kids to stop interrupting?

They have a plan. If someone interrupts, the parents don't answer, but do give the nonverbal reminder to wait. If the child can wait, she gets a positive reinforcement, like a hand on the shoulder, a hug, or a kiss. If the child doesn't wait, the parent tries one more time. If that one gets ignored, the child's request goes "to the back of the line" while the child sits separately from the group.

"How long did it take to teach your kids to do this?" I asked. "Well," the dad replied, "we're still working on it." Based on my own experience, and some child development research, I added a step to this. Here is how to cure interrupting:

1. Ask your child to stop and listen for a moment. Are you talking to someone or on the phone?

2. If you are busy, your child can place her hand on your arm. She should leave it there, gently.

3. You will put your hand over her hand. This lets her know that you are aware she needs your attention and are just waiting for a break in your conversation to speak to her.

4. As soon as you can, get to her question.

5. If your child doesn't do this to get your attention, do not respond. Just give him *the look*.

Parents, educators, autism support specialists, and even store managers have all told me this worked for their kids (and staff). This is a way to teach your child to get her needs met, and also teach her to interrupt respectfully.

Nonresponse can, with a clear explanation beforehand (see Chapter 52), help to solve a lot of unpleasant behaviors, like:

- Interrupting

- Whining

- Tantrums

- Talking back

- Sarcasm

- Teasing

- Demanding

Nonresponse is useful for kids as well as adults. We want to teach our children the ability to step away from conflict. Most kids naturally are inclined to respond, even to poor behavior. As we talked about in Chapter 39, it takes two people to engage for conflict to happen. With siblings or peers, kids can avoid a lot of these behaviors:

- Bickering

- Teasing

- Competition

- Fighting

- Gossiping

- Bullying

Imagine our daughter is at recess, and a girl who sees her standing waiting for the swings decides to bother her. "Your haircut is stupid and nobody likes you!" One of the most effective ways to stop that nastiness in its tracks is for your daughter to turn, raise her eyebrows at the girl, smile, and say nothing. Absolutely nothing. Because that is a clear message. Nonresponse avoids a lot of conflict, and can very often chastise more effectively than words. For kids to have this skill as one of the tools available to them, they need to know how to use it.

On purpose or not, we teach our kids a lot about how to manage conflict. We teach them how and when to argue, we teach them how they should expect to be treated by other people, and we teach them what types of communication are acceptable. Our children will try out a huge variety of interactions with us. When they try one that is not acceptable to you, make that clear. Then use nonresponse as a constant reminder that certain types of communication are not welcome and won't get an answer.

57

Separation: We Now Interrupt Our Regularly Scheduled Programming ...

Picture your child at the age of 14. Waiting for a bus, another teen he's never met sarcastically says, "Nice shoes." Recognizing this for the insult it is, your son gives his best "whatever" expression and turns his face away. The kid persists. "Seriously, d'you buy those? Or find 'em in the trash?" Your son responds with the current slang version of "Up yours." But this kid is looking for a fight. He approaches, "How about I put it up yours?" At this point, your son has two choices: engage or walk away. Teach him the value of separation when a situation takes an unexpected turn for the worse.

Separation can help kids change behavior. Separation can give children a chance to rethink, calm down, and be distracted from a strong emotion enough to get it under control. This doesn't mean kids like time-outs or being asked to play in a different room. The point isn't for them to see the value of the life lesson every time, but the parent should. Change the venue to encourage a change in attitude.

Time-outs.

- **Toddlers and preschoolers.** For two- and three-year-olds, separation usually means giving them a time-out. Just to review, this means a short period of time in a contained space out of view of computer or TV (because I don't think there is a child alive with the self-restraint

ASK·DOCTOR G

Parent Q: How do I know if my toddler is old enough for time-outs?

Well of course that depends on the child, but here's a tip: when your child starts doing things just to see what *you* will do, that's the right time to start showing her what you will do.

For example, each of our sons has proven this to us in the exact same way. We have dogs, and the dogs have a water bowl. Every one of our babies has crawled straight to that water bowl to splash, play, and, if we're not fast enough, drink. We pulled them away, told them no, distracted them. No problem. One day, though, each child has crawled to the water bowl and then looked right at me (or his father) and watched *us* while extending a hand toward the bowl. The look in their eyes absolutely says "So? Whatcha gonna do?" *That* is the cue that your child is ready to learn "when I do this thing I know I'm not allowed to do, then my parent does this other thing that I don't like."

So are you getting *that look* yet?

to not watch) and without toys. The point of this time is to show the child that the thing she was doing right before this was not OK. Many parents use this time to let their kids calm down. However, some kids do not calm down during this time; they get more worked up. If that is your child, time-outs may not work for her.

Some kids can stay where you tell them to without physical restraint. "Go sit on the bench." I have also heard the one minute for each year of their age formula. It's OK to be flexible. If they just need a minute to disengage and alter their behavior, then a minute is enough. Warning: Not having a set time can lead to the little one spending way longer than he needed to in the time-out spot, just because I (ahem) got distracted.

Some kids will not stay in one spot for a time-out no matter what you do. I do not suggest locking these kids in a room, though

I understand why you might be tempted. For little ones, a pack-and-play or crib is a good safe space for a minute or three. I have also heard the advice that kids should not use the same place for time-outs that they use for sleep. If you have a child with big sleep issues, that may be good advice for you. In general, I don't think kids have trouble making the distinction between sleep and trouble. For those kids who will climb down, out, or over rather than sit for a minute, you may have to sit with them on your lap and actually hold them in place. It is reasonable to gently restrain a child whose body is ahead of her brain by sitting with her on your lap and hugging her over her arms for a minute. Don't talk during this time or engage. Just be quiet for a minute as you sit with her.

- **Age 5–7.** This is still a good behavior reminder for kids in early elementary school. A second-grader probably does not need seven minutes on the bottom step, but just the opportunity to reset his mood or actions after a moment or two.

- **Ages 8–12.** Older kids stop benefiting from time-outs, usually around middle or older elementary school. The truth is, the concept still works, but the name is so baby-ish that sending them to a "time-out" will send your argument spiraling in a whole new "You treat me like a baby!" spin, complicating the situation.

Grown-ups can definitely benefit from time-out. I have a dear friend who will tell her kids (ages five and eight), "Now Mommy needs a time-out." Then she goes to her room to take a little time for herself. This can help your attitude and alter your behavior (even without wine). Don't underestimate the value of separation for yourself. As long as your kids are safe, they may be safer still if you get five minutes of uninterrupted time. You do not get to take a minute for each year of *your* age, unfortunately.

One suggestion about this technique: If you have a child who likes to think of herself as the grown-up, don't call your break a time-out. Call it a break or personal time or a Calgon-moment, but don't call it the same thing you use for them. Why? If you say to a child who often tries to be the boss that "Mommy needs a time-out …" well, you can't be surprised when that child decides to give you a time-out for interrupting.

"Back to your corners ..."

In a boxing match, when the fighting gets out of hand, the referee will say, "Back to your corners." This is a quick reminder of the rules and of what will and won't be tolerated, even in a fight. This works really well for sibling bickering and friend disagreements. This tactic can work at any age from toddler to 20. It may surprise you to observe that your four- and two-year-olds are actually sad when, after breaking up their fight for the third time in three minutes, you say, "OK. You two aren't playing nicely together just now. Mike, go play in your bedroom while Denee plays here for 10 minutes, and then you'll switch." Kids often really want to play together even if we feel it's "not going well." However, that makes it easier next time to encourage better behavior. Even older kids don't like enforced separation (kids don't usually like enforced anything), but it teaches valuable lessons. The most important lesson is: our home needs to be a safe place.

Use this technique when your home has become unpleasant for one or more of the people in it. That could mean you are stopping physical abuse (fighting), verbal abuse, or emotional abuse. When kids are bickering and it's not bothering either of them, go back to your own corner to think a minute about whether it is the best idea to intervene. Remember that kids practice on each other. With friends and siblings they practice criticizing, disagreeing, and blowing off steam. They are actually pretty good at letting each other know when a line has been crossed. These skills (both expressing negative emotions and stopping someone who is treating them poorly) will serve them well as adults.

What about when your child's friend is over and the two of them are having trouble getting along? Separation for brief periods of time is a great answer, especially when you don't want to punish someone else's kid. This is a way to hit the reset button. And most kids are happy to play with someone else's stuff by themselves for a while. After a certain age, you should not be intervening when your child has friends over unless they ask you to or you feel it's gotten dangerous in some way. For most kids, that age is middle elementary school.

Does separation work for tweens? Yes. This can be a natural consequence of rude behavior. However, use this sparingly. Most tweens need more family time and exposure, not less. Most tweens have an inner dialogue at the ready that sounds like this: "I don't care about being with these people anyway. They don't understand anything and don't care about me and I don't think they're even my real family. I wish I lived somewhere else." Using separation as a consequence isolates kids who are already feeling isolated.

What about "play" fighting?

When my boys fight (only hourly) I have to decide if it is for sport or in anger. If it is for sport, I don't intervene. If it is in anger, I do. How do I tell the difference? Sometimes I call a time-out and ask each boy "fun or scary?" If everyone says fun, time-in. When someone gets hurt (pretty much every time), no one gets in trouble since everyone had informed consent. This excludes anyone under four—they're not verbal enough for informed consent, and the older ones know they have to protect small children. We've taught the boys to "tap out" if they need the action to stop; they hit the ground twice or tap the other guy on the shoulder twice. It's worth noting that some boys do not like this puppy fighting and some girls do like it. Wrestling and tussling have more to do with personalities than gender. Make sure to help your children respect their own desires and those of others.

Separation is one of the keys to not being the parent you hate. Remember the main goal of separation: a cooling off period that allows the situation to change for the better. Don't underestimate the use of this when you are close to the end of your patience. Feel the frustration bubbling up? Hear yourself screaming? Let your child know that the situation is not yet resolved but that you need some time to think. Separate for a little while so that you can parent after making a calm decision. That is leading by example. Also, that is a way to avoid the look on your spouse's face when he or she returns from work to find you building a dog house in the backyard because you told your 12-year-old this is where she will be sleeping until she leaves for college.

58

Reminding: Did You Do That Yet?

Reminding is the most frequently used tool in my parenting toolkit. It can be a hammer, a wrench, or a screwdriver. However I use it, this is the best way I know to prevent having to use bigger, heavier tools later. But I get really tired of repeating myself, so I've learned to look at reminding a little more creatively.

There is nothing weak or lazy about needing reminders. Do you keep lists? Put notes on a calendar or in your phone? Are you a Post-It king? My husband even uses his label-maker for reminders. There are lots of deadlines, tasks, and events to keep in mind, and kids need to learn all the different ways to help them remember their stuff and their obligations.

Reminding our kids of what they need to do does not have to mean nagging. What's the difference? Tone and repetition. If you have to repeat something more than once, you will get annoyed and your child will hear the frustration louder than the words. Or she will learn to tune you out. So you can decide, right here and now, to never repeat something more than once ever again. Except if you're ordering drive thru; those speaker systems are terrible.

Repeat it back.

Before I went to medical school, I worked as a professional stage manager. That is the person in a theatrical production who, among a host of other duties, tells the actors when to go onstage. And because actors are often disorganized, inattentive, easily distracted, and busy (why yes, it did prepare me for parenting, how did you know?), stage managers give several "calls" before curtain. "Thirty minutes please." I would call into each dressing room at 7:30 p.m. six nights a week. The tradition in live theater is that the performers call back, "Thirty minutes, thank you." This serves two purposes: (1) the stage manager doesn't have to wonder if she was heard, and (2) the actor, who is contractually obligated to be onstage on time, can't later claim to have not heard the warning.

As a mom, I have shamelessly stolen this method. When we are getting ready to leave the house, or to stop a fun activity, I give my kids time calls. And they know they must repeat that call back to me. "We're leaving in five minutes, guys!" "OK, Mom, five minutes!" This solves a whole bunch of problems. Can you picture that shocked and angry look your child gives you when you announce you're actually leaving the playground and he never heard the first six times you said you were leaving in a few minutes? Completely avoid that.

Teach your kids to answer with some paraphrase of your request any time you ask them to do something. This can eradicate every argument your kids give about being ready for school on time, or washing up for dinner. There will be no "I didn't hear you" whines about turning off the computer, or turning off the light for bed.

Share the work.

Reminding can build kids' responsibility and resilience, or it can undermine them. If we use reminding as a tool that we model and teach our kids, it will help them meet their obligations and problem solve when they face new routines or challenges. If, however, we allow our kids to depend on our constant reminders and repetition, they will not learn to do their jobs without us or to overcome the challenges of getting work accomplished on their own. So, instead of being your child's alarm, calendar, to-do list, and assignment notebook, teach them to set and listen to other reminders.

Toddlers.

➤ **Pictures are great reminders.** Just ask any preschool teacher; a picture is worth a thousand nagging words. Put a picture of a knocking hand on doors that are often closed, like bathrooms and bedrooms. This will remind your child to be respectful of peoples' privacy without needing a reminder.

➤ **Move objects to help you remember a job.** Can your toddler take off a wet diaper in the morning and put on a dry pull up? Sure. Will he remember? He's more likely to if you put the garbage pail on the pull up box and put both next to the bed or the bedroom door.

Preschoolers.

➤ **Follow the numbers for bathroom jobs.** In Chapter 19, we talked about using scrapbook numbers to help kids remember all of their hygiene tasks in the bathroom. If you try this, you are teaching your child the same lesson that the lab in my office uses when they systematize work that needs to be done correctly, in the same order every time for safety.

➤ **A library book box.** As a kid I loved the library. As an adult I kind of dread it, because we have a bunch of books already, and it's hard for my kids to remember to keep the books separate. Then it's impossible to find the things before they're due, or even after. So take a milk crate or cardboard box and decorate it with your child. Put a big sign on it that says "Library Books" and leave it somewhere that a lot of reading happens. If a library book is not in someone's hand, it goes in the box.

Ages 5–7.

➤ **The list.** It is time to teach your child the magical powers of a good list. This is easier than you'd think because most kids love to check things off. Ask your child to make a list of all of the things she needs and wants to do in the morning before school. Be as specific as possible. You can take pictures of each of these things for a beginning reader. You can laminate the list or put it on a white board so she can scratch through what she's done. List-making is one of the best reminding tools kids can learn.

➤ **Got a screen time limit?** Get a timer and put it near the computer or TV. Teach your child to set it before starting to play. If it goes off and he stops on his own, that is great. If it goes off and he keeps playing, he loses a little time the next day.

Ages 8–10.

➤ **An assignment notebook.** If your school doesn't require this item yet, get one anyway. Quick, before kids' schoolwork gets the better of them, teach your child to write down anything a teacher says is going to happen. Homework, quizzes, tests, gym days (for sneakers), bring in a band instrument, a field trip permission form, PJ day at school—everything. Then teach her the habit of showing you the notebook each night, and figuring out what it means she needs to do. If you can build this skill before middle school, your child will be way ahead of the game.

➤ **Raise a weather kid.** Make it part of your bedtime routine to ask your child to check the weather each evening before bed (on your phone, on the computer, on TV, even in the newspaper—whatever works). Then think about what that means for the next day. Now teach the skill of advanced planning.

- Going to be sunny? Take the sunscreen and stick it in your sandal for the next morning.

- Rainy? Put an umbrella over the doorknob.

- Freezing? Snowing? Stick regular shoes in your backpack and set out your boots.

Ages 11–12.

➤ **Time for the reminder of all reminders—the alarm clock.** Transition out of being your child's alarm clock, just when she is transitioning into being a grumpy waker-upper. Get your child an alarm clock and teach her to use it. If she runs late, she'll need to set the alarm for that much earlier the next day until she finds a formula that works for her.

➤ **The phone reminder.** Even the most basic phones come with a calendar and alarm system. If you don't yet allow your child to have a phone for communication, you still might want to give him an old, not-connected-to-the-network phone. Library books due in two weeks? Teach him to put an alarm in the calendar. Likewise for soccer games (add in "bring uniform and ball and water bottle"), picture day, and any other important events. Teach him the value of putting lots of specifics in, like "procedure for science fair due, get supplies for experiment." Help him see the usefulness of putting alarms in *before* the due date; for example, "Mom's birthday in one week—buy really awesome gift and make heartfelt card by hand."

We have to remind our kids of their obligations, their events, and their tasks. When we slowly transition them into reminding themselves, and using the tools at hand, we are making them stronger. This means, of course, that they won't need us to nag them, which can feel like a loss to parents. Even harder, it means that we have to let their reminders fail them and not jump in. It's this hard parenting work that will teach our kids to be responsible and resilient. Take heart, though. Not being the "reminders" leaves us more time to have fun and meaningful interactions with our kids.

59

Rights vs. Privileges

So what if none of the previous ideas have worked? You've tried saying no, and meaning it. You (and your partner) have picked one behavior to work on, discussed it as a family, and you've been as consistent as a normal human being can be. You told your child exactly what you expect and detailed the behavior you're hoping for. You've done your best to let life teach the lesson. You've tried not responding, separating your child for a while, reminding, remorse.... And none of it is working. You're in the right chapter.

Now it's time to take a step back and figure out what your child wants and needs.

We believe our kids have certain rights. Most of us would agree that they have a right to food, shelter, clothes, education, health care, and love. In no circumstances would we intentionally deprive a child under the age of 13 of any of these basic human needs, no matter his behavior. Much as my kids might wish otherwise, we're just not going to say, "You've behaved so badly that we're cancelling your doctor's appointment!"

OK, we've established that our kids are entitled to certain things from us. Everything else? Everything else is a privilege. Everything. Privileges have to be earned and can be lost. Privileges depend on good behavior, and following the rules.

Talk to your parenting partner. Make a list of everything you feel is a right for the kids in your home. This might vary by child. For example, you might have a child who struggles to read. You would never take away that child's reading time or library trips because he needs the encouragement. On the other hand, you might have a child (like mine) with whom you know you can make a huge impression by taking away pleasure reading time. Perhaps one of your kids is not getting enough exercise. You would never tell her that you refuse to drive her to soccer practice; that would not help her learn to be the active person you want her to be. It's also possible that you would include spiritual learning on your list of rights, as very few faith-based families will "ground" a child from going to services or Sunday school. So now you have a catalog of items that you will keep separate and protected from the long list of privileges you might take away from your child.

Next, it's time to make a much longer inventory of all the things your child has, or does, or that you do for your child that aren't a necessity. Everything that doesn't fall on the list of what you agree he needs goes on the list of stuff he just wants. Those are the motivators to get him out of his comfort zone and into better behavior.

Once we know what aspects of our kids' lives are privileges, we know what we can remove without harming him. Be clear about the long list of things that can fill in this blank: "If you do that again, I will need to take away your _____ until you've shown me better behavior."

Toddlers.

➤ **Toys.** All of the toys that she loves are privileges. Set aside the one stuffed animal, blanket, or other love object she uses for comfort (since love is one of the rights we want to protect); every other item she plays with is fair game to remove.

➤ **Activities.** Play time, arts-and-crafts, games, extended bath time, stories at bedtime; these playtime activities are wonderful. If a poor behavior is connected to a particular activity, like breaking art supplies and having art time, then that art time is sacrificed.

➤ **Outings.** Going to the playground, library, gym, neighbor's house, or whatever the next plan was can be tied to behavior right now.

Preschoolers.

➤ **Toys.** As kids get a little older, they can understand that their possessions are important to them but not to us parents. We show them that behavior earns good rewards or struggle when we say, "You can earn this back today ... or next week."

➤ **Activities.** Playdates are usually the most exciting event in a preschooler's day. Expecting your child to be a good listener ties in really well to having a friend over or being allowed to go to someone else's home.

➤ **Outings.** It's still important to keep consequences as close as possible to the time of the behavior you're trying to change. So if the outing was part of your plan for today, then be clear: "Because you're choosing to do this thing I've asked you not to do, we're not going to be able to go to _____."

Ages 5 to 7.

➤ **Toys.** As children enter the age of reason, they might keep track of who gave them something. So, if you hear "You can't take that away, it was a gift from Grandma!" don't be alarmed. Praise your child for remembering the source of the gift, and then let her know that of course you can take that away. Your roof, your rules.

➤ **Activities.** Playing with our children is a great way to show love. We also show love by enforcing our boundaries. If a child is, for example, being disrespectful to you or a sibling, then he might not get to participate in game night. In addition to encouraging better behavior, you're teaching him that we shouldn't play with people who treat us poorly.

➤ **Outings.** When kids behave poorly at home, we often can't wait to get them out the door to an extracurricular activity. Those same hobbies, though, can be great motivators for kids to improve behavior. "If you want to continue with basketball, you'll need to get your chores done before practice. Otherwise you'll need the extra time at home to clean the bathroom."

Ages 8 to 10.

➤ **Toys.** If you're not totally sure what your child's "toys" are now, just watch how she spends her home time. Whatever takes her attention is of value to her, and is a privilege she needs to keep earning by improving her behavior.

➤ **Activities.** Friends are taking on more and more importance in your elementary schooler's life. Spending time with friends is important, but not as important as learning to follow your rules. Help your child understand that he can earn or lose this time through his choices.

➤ **Outings.** We want our kids to explore the world and learn about being with others. However, it can help children to spend more time at home, especially when they are having a difficult time with boundaries and rules.

Ages 11 to 12.

➤ **Toys.** Our middle schoolers have more gadgets than toys. These are still privileges. Even if a child spent all her own money on that tablet, the Internet connectivity is still your domain. A great Post-It that a parent left for his kids each morning in the summer: "Want today's Wi-Fi password? Walk the dog, fold the laundry, clean the kitchen, then we'll talk."

➤ **Activities.** Hopefully your tween is making most of his own plans. But that ride to the mall, the carpool you drive, the sleepovers you allow, all of those are privileges.

➤ **Outings.** Hold family time separate, as this is part of keeping our kids connected to us. All other outings, though—from weekend activities to movies with friends or shopping excursions—are great-behavior-dependent.

These kinds of consequences take repetition and perseverance. Any character traits we want to instill in our kids we must demonstrate ourselves. We'll need creativity, empathy, diligence, and strength. Sometimes we have to take away a bunch of privileges to make our kids genuinely uncomfortable. That discomfort is necessary to change behavior. People don't change behavior unless we truly believe either

1. It will make me happier, or

2. I *have* to.

Raising kids is hard work. Taking things away from them, grounding them, and denying them their (at that moment) heart's desires all takes a lot of willpower. Even worse? Our kids will make it as hard on us as they know how. That seems easier to them than changing behavior. Go back to the consistency chapter, though. Kids will fight back against the consequence only if they think they can change our minds. Once they realize that we really mean it, then we can begin to see change.

Refusing a child something he wants (especially when it's in our power to give it) is maybe the hardest thing to do as a parent. If you're feeling guilty, look at your reason. Are you refusing it out of anger? Laziness? Spite? Only refuse it if it will help reach your big goal: to raise a child who has the character and skills needed to be a great adult.

60

Keep Your Focus Positive

So how can we talk about refusing and reminding and remorse and still be the parents we want to be? How can we be fun, warm, loving, and supportive if we're using all of these tough tools in response to our kids' behavior? It's all in the attitude. Our attitudes.

You know boundaries are good for your kids. You know love is good for them, too. When I ask parents about "the parent they hate" they tell me of going to bed feeling like all they did was yell. Parents lament scolding and refusing all day long. They wish there had been some laughing, some smiles, some hugs but it just didn't happen. Tomorrow is a new day! Just as we can control the plan we put in place for our kids' behaviors, we can plan our own behavior as well.

For your child (of any age), consider all these while you discipline:

- **Who.** Make sure that only the child or children who misbehaved hear about it from you. The temptation is great to teach all the kids within the sound of our voice the lesson, but that never works. Each child has to learn from his own experiences, so don't waste your time or ruin your family's day trying to make everyone suffer for one person's bad choice.

- **What.** Give the consequence as soon as you can so that the whole experience doesn't drag on for everyone. Even if your child is grounded for a week, that doesn't mean he is allowed no joy or laughter in his life. Make the terms clear and then allow for the day to still be a good one, even with the restriction in place.

- **When.** If it's possible, choose the consequence and get it over with as soon as you can. This allows a child (especially a young one) to make the connection from behavior to consequence clearly. Also, it gets to the best part faster—the reconciliation. I'll talk more about that in the last chapter, but this is the time when your child will really get to feel your love, and you'll both feel better.

- **Where.** When you guide your child's behavior, try to do it as respectfully as you can. Using shame by chastising them in front of friends, or in public, often causes kids to lose the lesson you're trying to teach in the wave of embarrassment they feel. So get your child alone, or be as private and respectful as possible. Just lowering your voice really gets a child's attention. You'll have a much greater impact.

- **How.** Be just as calm and rational as you can. For me, that is not always so calm or so rational, but it's always my goal. The more matter of fact I can be with my child about his poor behavior, the easier it is for him to believe that I still love him. When we correct our kids, our words are not all "I love you." But our tone of voice can be. At least some of the time!

- **Why.** Limit your bad mood or frustration as best you can. If your child's poor behavior made you feel inadequate or angry or hurt, give yourself a break and try to shake it off before getting back to whatever else is going on. This models resilience for your kids and makes sure that one tough interaction doesn't ruin the whole day.

If you feel your own attitude worsening, reach for one of your own resilience tools. Talk to a friend, or grab a cool beverage. Exercise or surf the web for a few minutes. As long as your kids are safe, you definitely help them by taking a quick break to improve how you're feeling.

Take control of the words you say in your head. If you are repeating "They never listen, I have to do everything!" you will for sure have a bad day. Try saying instead, "I've got this!" or "That was hard, but we can have a good day." This internal monologue is not a trick, it's a key to success.

It is completely possible to guide a child's behavior and still see that you both can have a good day. It's the absolute truth that we can't control how someone else feels. It's also true that, as the parent of a young child, we have a lot of power over her mood and behavior—when we control our own.

61

Surprising Consequences

The word "consequences" has mostly replaced the word "punishment." Some of that is probably due to our cultural squeamishness regarding unhappy children. I do punish my kids. However, I also search for consequences that will surprise and amaze them. I encourage you to do the same.

When you consider the behavior you are trying to change, get creative with ways to flip that undesirable action (not your child) on its head. Of course, we have to model the conduct we want from our kids, but it can make an even stronger impression if we can get the child to show herself the better behavior as an effect of our consequences. In this way our kids get to experience the surprising, and often heartwarming, results of doing the right thing.

Toddlers.

➤ Turn hits into pats. Little kids hit out of anger and frustration, and also sometimes from excitement. If your young child is too aggressive toward you (or a sibling, or even a pet), grab a pillow. Show your child a hit to the pillow, or a gentle pat to the arm. Give your child the choice by pointing to the pillow and asking, "Hit?" and then pointing to your arm and asking, "Or pat?" You are respecting your child's emotion without allowing painful or damaging behavior.

Preschoolers.

➤ When his friend is over, your preschooler does not want to be bothered by a younger sibling. You might be inclined to force the kids to play together, but it's also possible to ask the older kids to put on a "show" for the younger ones. This can teach a strong lesson and makes for a great experience for everyone.

Ages 5–7.

➤ At dinner one of your kids says something unkind to a sibling. Instead of chastising that child, ask her to find three things that she really respects about that same sibling.

Ages 8–10.

➤ One of your kids wants to invite a friend over that has in the past ignored your family's rules and encouraged your own child to behave poorly. Instead of banning that child from your home, ask your child for an action plan to avoid the problem for this next proposed playdate. How will you or he talk to the friend about it, and what should the consequences be if the rules are broken?

Ages 11–12.

➤ Your tween sits through a family event but is totally disengaged, texting or playing a solitary game and completely missing the point of Grandma's birthday dinner. Challenge your child to plan the next family event (including Grandma) in a way that will make her feel honored and valued and be fun for the kids.

Turn the tables on your child's actions. This is a great alternative, especially for those moments when you're frustrated with punishing!

62

Admire Your Kids

Our kids usually know what we want them to do better. It's not so hard to remember the last thing you got in trouble for doing, or a time when you were recently scolded. That experience leaves a particular feeling in your stomach, and the same is true for our children. Part of "not being the parent I hate" is balancing out that feeling with genuine praise.

Praise is mighty when it gives a person power. You have the power to make your child walk taller, stand strong, and believe in her own worth. So how can we find the right words and the right time to tell our kids about their awesomeness?

Healthy praise.

- **Focuses on action, not talent.** Praising a child's natural ability or talent teaches her that this is what you value most. Also, this dampens a child's willingness to try something new or challenging, as she might not be naturally excellent at the new skill. What happens if even a hugely gifted athlete moves up in competitive level? Eventually she will not be the best in the group. That child is praiseworthy for the effort she puts forth, far more than the gift she was born possessing.

- **Does not exaggerate.** Increasing a child's self-esteem does not happen by amplifying praise. Develop a child's confidence by helping him see the improvements he has made or the value of his actions.

- **Does not excuse poor behavior.** The urge is strong to praise our kids after we punish them in an effort to build them back up. However, kids need that period of remorse to internalize the consequences of poor behavior. Don't thwart the process by jumping in with pats and strokes because you feel bad when your child feels bad. Let him earn your praise before you offer it.

- **Is one person's opinion.** We often use praise in an attempt to change our child's point of view. "You *are* great at math!" This type of argument does not convince him and can have the opposite effect. Instead, try saying, "I admire your hard work in math class."

- **Is honest.** We do not benefit our children by lying to them with praise. Kids are often more self-aware than we think. For all the reasons we should never lie to our children, lying to them about their skills or abilities can be especially damaging to our child and our relationship. The phrase "You can do anything you want to do" is, for example, not actually true. So how do we build our kids up if that is what we tell them?

- **Builds internal motivation.** Internal motivation means doing the right or good thing for your own reasons. It takes kids a while to notice how great they feel when they put forth extra effort and improve at something. Praise should strive to reinforce that feeling, not replace it by teaching kids only to look to others to say if an action was worthwhile.

There are so many ways and times to praise our kids. Here are a few ways to commend kids for some of their great actions.

Ways to praise.

- **Catch them doing good.** We have to notice and speak up when our kids misbehave. Surprise them by noticing—out loud—when they overcome an obstacle or try a challenge or act kindly. It's strengthening for our kids to know that we are watching and admiring their good work.

- **Great gossip.** Have you ever noticed that an overheard compliment can feel more genuine and substantial than positive feedback given directly to you? It's definitely worthwhile to say to a child, "I admire how you help us protect your baby brother." If your child has done something excellent, take the time to tell the story, in his hearing, to a teacher, grandparent, or friend. Then he will really know how much you value his act.

- **Thank heavens for the good stuff.** If you pray, pray about your kids. Speak out loud the strong behaviors you've admired that day or that week, and you will help your child see the power of her actions in your esteem.

- **Write a birthday letter.** I have never pulled off the milestone calendars or baby books or other record-every-moment products that exist to document our kids' lives. The one tradition I can manage (even if I run a few months behind) is a letter, once a year, to each of our children about what we most admire about him that year. This kind of praise, that a child can take out and read when he needs it, then put away for later, can serve as a reminder of our admiration when his faith in himself flags.

- **Play "I admire …"** Teach all of your kids the power of praise as a relationship builder. At dinner, ask each person to say one thing she admires that someone else in the family does. When we do this, I'm always surprised by what my kids notice.

Let's imagine someone asked your child, "What does your Mom or Dad like most about you?" Does she know? Can he name three things you think are spectacular about his actions? Won't it feel great for both of you when he can?

63

The Power of Love

Praise can be overblown, inflated, and even damaging to a child's self-esteem if we overdo it. You know what can't be overdone? Love. Our kids need the rock solid certainty of our love so that they can venture out, try, fail, and start the cycle again. The more certain kids are of our love, the more they can try to make the behavior changes we ask of them.

1. Intention.

Love is why you picked up this book. Unless you're only reading as a favor to me (thanks Dad), you have the love to be intentional in your parenting. You are looking for ideas and suggestions to make your family even stronger. You are willing to search out new ways to raise your child to be his or her best self.

When we demonstrate that intentionality to our kids, they see the love. Every conversation we have about parenting, every resource we seek to test out, our kids know that we take this child-rearing thing seriously. At that family meeting when you explain about the new no-whining policy, you are showing your kids that you love them enough to work on them. Boundaries are intentional, and a concrete symbol of our love.

2. Patience.

"Love is patient." Wow, not my love. I am so impatient, my husband bought me a clock with the word NOW in place of every number. He has shown me, however, that being patient is a tangible way to demonstrate my love to my children. Even just a bit of patience allows us to

- Play a game.

- Wait before deciding a punishment.

- Appreciate effort rather than results.

- Notice small improvements.

- Let a child finish his story. Or even his sentence.

3. Empathy.

Showing genuine empathy when we have to make a child uncomfortable is one of the ways we demonstrate our love. That love allows us to consider a child's point of view. When we seriously consider a child's point of view, we don't need to change the consequence but we can open her up to guidance and teaching.

My son is running around our wood-floored living room in his sock feet. I've asked him already to stop running or remove his socks. I've explained that the laws of physics enforce themselves; he's going to crash and it's going to hurt. When he crashes, the temptation to scold him immediately, over his crying, is strong. The problem is, he can't learn from me if I ignore his pain. First he needs to know that I hear he hurt himself. He needs to know I care, and that I've checked to make sure it isn't serious. Then he is able (although not happy) to hear about the connection and learn a lesson.

I've never been a big fan of the old cliché: This is going to hurt me more than it's going to hurt you. I call B.S. on that; punishing a child has the biggest effect on that child, and it should. However, we can have genuine empathy for a child's unhappiness. No matter what choices our kids make, we love them. No matter what consequences they face, we feel for them. That feeling is what allows us to ground a child and then mean it when we say, "I am truly sorry that you can't go to the birthday party. I hope next time you make a better choice with your behavior."

4. Strength.

Tell your kids you love them. Hug them and kiss them (as long as they don't mind the kissing), send them lunch notes or texts, or use a secret code. Our kids need to hear about our love. Now let them feel the true strength of your love. That power allows you to do what your kids need, even when it's not what they want.

Keep your eye on the big picture. Only you (and hopefully one or two other adults) love that child enough to teach the hard lessons, to hold those boundaries. Be strong in the limits you set on your kids' behavior. Be certain enough of your love that you don't have to "prove it" by giving in. You can prove it by holding firm.

5. Reconciliation.

There is no more teachable moment than that reconnection after a child misbehaves and lives through the consequence. Don't use this moment to hammer home the lesson you wanted to teach about his behavior! Use this moment to teach something even more important: that your love is constant.

Here is something that shocks a preschooler: You still love her when you're mad. You love her when she misbehaves. You love her when she doesn't listen. You love her when she's disrespectful. Your love does not depend on what she does or how she behaves: it just is. This is so strange to kids that they need to learn this lesson over and over again.

Reconciliation is more than just a great feeling. A broken bone repairs itself with extra protection at the point of the break. When a relationship is hurt by one person's behavior, and there is a consequence, reconciliation is the healing of that hurt. When your child apologizes, or completes a time-out, or stays home from the birthday party ... let him feel your love. It will heal both of you.

6. Attention.

This is the strongest expression of our love for our kids. Words matter, and kids benefit from hearing "I love you." But words are hard for some to say, or to hear. And words are not enough. So ...

- Sit on the floor and play (this reminder is for me).
- Listen to the joke ... for the 12th time today. Or teach her a new one.
- Learn the names of all the stuffed animals.
- Read the story.
- Go to the game.

- Watch the silly movie.

- Chaperone the field trip.

- Drive the carpool.

- Sit down to dinner.

- Cuddle at bedtime.

- And if you're away … call, and listen.

Kids need our love in all of its forms. Love encourages us to notice our kids' behavior. Love strengthens us to parent them the best we know how. Love enables us to discipline our children, and to reconcile with them after they understand the consequences of their actions. Love is how we get the energy to do all this hard parenting work. And love is why all this work is worth it.

Conclusion: You Know What You Want

You are the parenting expert on your kids. You have dreamed over who your child may become. You've thought about who this person is, and what he is capable of doing. You have struggled with her personality and outlook. You've rejoiced in his unique perspective and abilities. You have discussed—sometimes endlessly—how and what and when to do with your child. You have lost sleep caring for this human. You have gotten to know these children as well as anyone in the whole world has, and probably better. Trust in that knowledge.

You deserve respect, and so do your kids. You are giving your children the unselfish gift of raising them. Know your worth and let your kids respect you by teaching them how. Help your children maneuver in the world to their own best advantage by showing them how to make others feel respected. Take the time to teach your kids meaningful ways to get the respect they deserve.

Responsibilities can build us up. The world is full of references to how we are weighed down by our tasks and obligations, but your kids will thrive with more responsibility than with fewer. Share the work, and push them to the leading edge of their potential as they strive to be "bigger" and more grown up. Gift your kids and yourself by letting them surprise the whole family with what they can accomplish.

Resilience is the best way to arm our children for all the challenges they will face. Bad things will happen. Protect your kids now by giving them lots of practice solving problems and surviving difficulty. We won't always be with our children, or even here for them as adults. This is the treasure you can pass on that will never fail your son or daughter. Resilience is perhaps the hardest thing to teach one we love, as it involves suffering. You love your kids enough to do this for them.

You have the power to make changes in your parenting life. In my medical practice, I often encourage people to make changes. Change is hard for everyone. Here is the secret I've learned, though: What parents will not do for themselves they will absolutely do for their children. A mom may not take a half hour to walk each day to improve her health, but she will take her son out and run with him every day at 5:00 a.m. A dad tells me for years that smoking "Isn't so bad," but when his daughter lights up he'll quit before he even comes in to see me for help.

You know what you want from your children, and for them. Knowledge and power are the ingredients necessary to get the behavior you want from your kids. That parent you hate to be? The one who feels powerless or angry, who yells or cries or withdraws? You now have the knowledge and the power to set that parent aside almost every time. And almost every time is enough.

Raise kids who know how to be respectful, responsible, and resilient. You will have adult children who can survive their challenges, meet their obligations, and reach their goals.

Acknowledgments

I must begin and end by thanking my husband, Noam, without whom nothing I want to accomplish would be possible, but *especially* writing a book! It was your idea that I do this (when I was more than skeptical); this is your baby as much as mine. Like our actual kids, you were there at the conception and delivery, and have worked as hard (though differently) as I during the gestation. And speaking of our kids, this book would genuinely not be possible without any of the four of you. You not only have been constantly experimented upon, you have actively contributed your opinions about what parents need to know. Thanks, guys, for your patience, energy, and love. I will help you achieve your dreams just as open-heartedly as you are helping me achieve mine. And yes, you may remind me I said that.

A cherished friend said that acknowledgments are not interesting to anyone not acknowledged therein, and noted that many folks read them anyway. If you are one of those people (as she and I both are), I beg your indulgence, and perhaps your forgiveness as well. It's like an Academy Awards speech with no orchestra to blame if you leave someone out.

The rest of this is in no particular order, as I have no idea how to prioritize gratitude.

Mom and Dad, I didn't credit you with enough while I was growing up. I get it now.

I've adopted a few more parents along the way. Ima, you are everything a daughter-in-law could hope for, truly. Ma B, you took me in, taught me, and kept me, and now you're a forever friend. Joe and Phyllis, I know you *tried* to have an only child. I'm glad you took us on anyway. Lia and Natan, thank you for your hearts.

Keren, thank you for helping us raise these boys. We love you.

Do you have friends that are family of your heart? We do, and are grateful for it.

Rachele and Dan, Mary, Josh and Sophie; I know it's all my fault, and I'm glad. Rachele, you are my not-so-silent partner in this, and every other, hare-brained scheme.

Vita and Jonathan, thank you for helping us create the recipe for this particular Kool-Aid. To you both and to Eitan, Akiva, and Adi, thank you for knowing that family is defined by those inside it, and for being inside ours.

Sharon and Aaron, and Noa, Roni, and Nadav, you are our community wherever you go. It wouldn't be complete without you.

Marisa and David, and Gib5on, for Shabbat dinners and Lego playdates and for taking a chance on a strange connection to build a really great friendship.

To Ken Ginsburg, MD, and Wendy Mogel, PhD, for inspiring and teaching me, and for being such tough acts to follow.

For all the women who have listened to, read, tested out, responded to, and encouraged these ideas, my sincere gratitude and love: Val, Michele, Amy, Deesha, Melissa, Jen, Lauren, Susan, Elana, Dani, and the couple of people who told me they didn't want their names in here.

You know what they teach you in medical school about starting a business? Nothing. To all of my mentors and accountability partners: The Women of DBA, Rachel, Sue, Abby, Elizabeth, Marisa, Erin, Alia, Jenn, Jennifer, Judy, Sarah, Ben, Shellyn, Stephanie, Gary, Henry, Danny, Elissa, Leni, Benj, Carpy, Willy, and Dad, and everyone I already mentioned, too. Everyone who loves me has helped!

Since med school teaches just as much about writing a book as about business, I thank sincerely Julia Pastore and the fantastic team at Demos Health. You all are generous of spirit as well as gifted in your work. This book simply would not be without you.

My doctoring home is the Squirrel Hill Health Center. Thank you to my mentors and colleagues there. Andrea and Susan, you have shown me what it means to be a working mom, and your flexibility and leadership make me a better doctor. There is no finer or more dedicated group assembled than the people I am honored to work with at SHHC. That includes, of course, my patients. Thank you for sharing your pain and joys and stories with me. I am honored to be a part of your life.

So many parents and educators have come to my acquaintance because of the speaking and writing I have been lucky enough to do. Thank you to all the members of my community. I hope when you read your stories in this book you will find that I have done them justice.

My heartfelt appreciation goes, today and every day, to Adora English and Jess Ponce of Media 2x3 for taking me under their wings and making it seem like this amazing trajectory was actually because of *my* work! It is rare to find friendship through business to the extent I have with both of you.

Remember I said I must begin and end with my husband? Noam, thank you for knowing what I need to do—often before I do—and never failing to push me to go for it. June 20, 2021, baby!

Index

About the Author

Deborah Gilboa, MD, aka "Dr. G," is a widely recognized parenting expert, family physician, international speaker, media authority, and (most fun but challenging of all) mom of four boys. She developed the "3 R's of Parenting" to empower parents to raise respectful, responsible, and resilient kids, in response to the years of character building questions she's received from her patients and Ask Doctor G community.

Dr. G is a monthly contributor on CBS' *Pittsburgh Today Live*, ABC's *Windy City Live*, WQED's *iQ SmartParent*, and appears regularly on news programs around the country. She contributes frequently to *Huffington Post, Parents, Your Teen* magazine, *Parents* magazine, and MSNBC.com. Dr. G is a Clinical Associate Professor at the University of Pittsburgh School of Medicine, where she received her medical degree, and a frequent lecturer at her alma mater, Carnegie Mellon University, where she received a BFA in drama.

She is also the author of *Teach Resilience: Raising Kids Who Can Launch!; Teach Responsibility: Empower Kids with a Great Work Ethic*; and *Teach Respect: That's My Kid!*—user-friendly parenting activity books designed for today's busy adults.

Dr. G and her husband are raising their four sons, and a couple of dogs, in beautiful Pittsburgh, Pennsylvania.

For more information and to connect with Dr. G, go to www.AskDoctorG.com.